Bah, Humbug!

Bah, Humbug!

GRUMPING THROUGH THE SEASON

WILLIAM COLE

St. Martin's Press

NEW YORK

Production Editor: David Stanford Burr
Design by Judith A. Stagnitto

Library of Congress Cataloging-in-Publication Data

Bah, humbug! / William Cole, editor.
        p.   cm.
    "A Thomas Dunne Book."
    ISBN 0-312-08279-7
    1. Christmas—Humor.   I. Cole, William, 1919–
PN6231.C36B3   1992
808.87'933—dc20   92-23843
                                  CIP

First Edition: November 1992

10 9 8 7 6 5 4 3 2 1

Acknowledgments

Every effort has been made to trace the ownership of all copyrighted material and to secure the necessary permissions to reprint these selections. In the event of any question arising as to the use of any material, the editor and the publisher, while expressing regret for any inadvertent error, will be happy to make the necessary correction in future printings.

Grateful acknowledgment is made to the following for permission to reprint the copyrighted material listed below:

Eleanor M. Bender for "Scrooge in a Manger" by Amy Clampitt. From *Open Places* #38/39.

Gerard Benson for "Lines for a Card" and "Hark" by Gerard Benson, Bradford, Yorkshire, UK.

Carcanet Press Ltd. for "The Computer's First Christmas Card" by Edwin Morgan. From *The Second Life* by Edwin Morgan, published by Edinburgh University Press, 1968.

William Cole for "St. Nick Is Too Thick" and "A Father's Thought" by William Cole.

Doubleday for "Christmas Greetings for 1923" from *So There!*, by Franklin P. Adams. Copyright © 1923

to reprint from *Mad Magazine*. Copyright © 1976 by E. C. Publications, Inc.

Bob McKenty for "Not so Calm, Not so Bright", "Naughty Santa!" and "Farewell, Noel" by Bob McKenty.

John Mella for "The Misanthrope's Christmas" by John Mella.

The National Review for "Why the Heaths Didn't Have This Year's Christmas Carol Program" by Aloïse Buckley Heath. Copyright © by National Review, Inc., 150 E. 35th Street, New York, NY 10016. Reprinted by permission.

Oberon Press for "Christmas Lights on Yonge Street" by Raymond Souster from *Collected Poems of Raymond Souster,* by permission of Oberon Press.

The Observer Ltd. for "Dear Father Christmas" by Russell Davies and "Dear Father Christmas" by Russell Davies from *New Statesman & Society*. Copyright © New Statesman & Society.

Omni Publications International, Ltd. for "Visions of Poly-Plums Dance in My Head" by Joy Nimnon Kraus and "Xmas Afterthought" by William Pratt from *The Bedside Phoenix Nest* published in 1965 issue of *Saturday Review*.

Penguin Books, Ltd., for "Christmas" from *Memories with Food at Gypsy House* by Felicity and Roald Dahl (Viking, 1991). Copyright © 1991 by the Estate of Felicity and Roald Dahl.

Louis Phillips for "Why it is so Difficult to Give an

Elephant as Gift for Christmas" and "Ode to My Bank Account on Christmas Day" by Louis Phillips, reprinted by permission of the author. "What's Your Christmas I.Q.?" by Louis Phillips, originally published in *Family Circle,* reprinted by permission of the author.

Random Century Group for "Mock Christmas Carol" from *Collected Poems 1980–1990* by Gavin Ewart. Published by Hutchinson.

Arthur Roth for "Treed!" by Arthur Roth.

Louise H. Sclove for "A True Bill Agaynst Christmasse" by Arthur Guiterman. Reprinted by permission of Louise H. Sclove.

John Sweetman for "A Fragment from a Mummer's Play" by John Sweetman. By permission of the author.

Rosemary Thurber for "A Farewell to Santa Claus (or, Violins are Nice for Boys with Chins)" and "A Visit from Saint Nicholas (in the Ernest Hemingway Manner)" by James Thurber. Copyright © 1989 Rosemary A. Thurber. From *Collecting Himself,* ed. by Michael J. Rosen, published by Harper & Row.

Watkins/Loomis Agency, Inc. for "Christmas Family Reunion" by Peter DeVries from *The Tents of Wickedness.* Copyright © 1949, 1950, 1952 by Peter DeVries. Reprinted by permission of the author and Watkins/Loomis Agency.

A. P. Watt Ltd. on behalf of Denis Norden for a prose parody based on "I'm Dreaming of a White Christmas" (Irving Berlin, title of song), excerpt from *The Complete and Utter "My Word!" Collections* by Denis Norden.

Contents

Introduction

*T*hey've already taken the Christ out of Christmas; now the time has come to emphasize the "No" in "Noel."

The first sentence in Alan Harrington's book *The Immortalist* has a bold elegance: "Death is an imposition on the human race and is no longer acceptable." A slight variation could easily apply to Christmas: "The Christmas season is an imposition on the adults of the human race and is no longer acceptable."

The annual orgasm takes place—takes over, rather—for a full month each year. The word in book publishing is, when December looms, "Forget it. Nothing gets done." My household god, H. L. Mencken, was severely annoyed if friends sent him presents, and in his early years expressed exasperation when his Germanic mother decorated the house. He called it all "Christmas blahs."

Roald Dahl admits to certain twinges of nostalgia for Christmas past, and I agree. I miss the joy of the children—but not the much encouraged greed. I miss the pungent smell of the Christmas tree—but of late growers have come up with a shapely tree that has no

smell whatsoever. I have always enjoyed the carols—
but not in such relentless succession. The contributors
to this jeremiad have said just about everything that
needs saying, so on to the experts, and

God help us, every one!

—WILLIAM COLE

Scrooge Was Right

"A merry Christmas, uncle! God save you!" cried a cheerful voice. It was the voice of Scrooge's nephew, who came upon him so quickly that this was the first intimation he had of his approach.

"Bah!" said Scrooge, "Humbug!"

He had so heated himself with rapid walking in the fog and frost, this nephew of Scrooge's, that he was all in a glow; his face was ruddy and handsome; his eyes sparkled, and his breath smoked again.

"Christmas a humbug, uncle!" said Scrooge's nephew. "You don't mean that, I am sure?"

"I do," said Scrooge. "Merry Christmas! What right have you to be merry? What reason have you to be merry? You're poor enough."

"Come, then," returned the nephew gaily. "What right have you to be dismal? What reason have you to be morose? You're rich enough."

Scrooge having no better answer ready on the spur of the moment, said, "Bah!" again; and followed it up with "Humbug."

"Don't be cross, uncle!" said the nephew.

"What else can I be," returned the uncle, "when I

live in such a world of fools as this? Merry Christmas! Out upon merry Christmas! What's Christmas time to you but a time for paying bills without money; a time for finding yourself a year older, but not an hour richer; a time for balancing your books and having every item in 'em through a round dozen of months presented dead against you? If I could work my will," said Scrooge indignantly, "every idiot who goes about with 'Merry Christmas' on his lips should be boiled with his own pudding, and buried with a stake of holly through the heart. He should!"

"Uncle!" pleaded the nephew.

"Nephew!" returned the uncle, sternly, "keep Christmas in your own way, and let me keep it in mine."

"Keep it!" repeated Scrooge's nephew. "But you don't keep it."

"Let me leave it alone, then," said Scrooge. "Much good may it do you! Much good it has ever done you!"

—CHARLES DICKENS
A Christmas Carol

I Loathe

Christmas

Christmas

I loathe Christmas.

Christmas is for children. Sixty-five and seventy years ago, when I was small, Christmas was entirely a family affair and very wonderful it was. The stocking was always hung at the end of the bed the night before and the next morning it would be filled with simple things, like an orange, some nuts, a tiny model Dinky car, a puzzle, some pencils and perhaps even a fountain pen. The main presents, never very expensive or elaborate, were wrapped up under the Christmas tree, and they were nearly all from the family. The toys were clockwork and we loved them. The Meccano sets were made of metal, not plastic. The jigsaw puzzles were cut from wood, not cardboard, the teddy bears were of wool, not poly-something-or-other, and the china dolls had eyes that shut when you laid them down. Nowadays all toys are battery-run, with remote-control gadgets and complex electronic mechanisms that go wrong after a week. Everything is expensive and full of silicon chips.

Christmas is also a time when a fair number of adults

who never go to church during the rest of the year go to morning service to sing jolly songs and pay their annual dues to Christianity. But basically Christmas has become an obscene festival, a bonanza for shop-keepers, who get rich at the expense of the rest of the population, who get poor.

Present-giving among adults has reached a ridicu-lous level. Long lists are compiled, not just of relatives and close friends, but of all sorts of acquaintances who you don't really care very much about. You live in fear that someone you've left out will give you a present and it will be too late to give one back. Everything has to be tit for tat, that is the golden rule: "I've got to get something for her because she always gives me one."

The saddest thing about all this is that it puts a very serious financial strain on many young single working people, who find it hard enough to make ends meet anyway. Suddenly, once a year, convention compels them to fork out their savings. I hate it.

A few sensible folk make no-present agreements with each other, and to my mind everyone outside the immediate family and close friends should do this.

Christmas cards are another racket. I agree it is nice to send a once-a-year greeting to an old and distant friend. But apart from that, even longer lists are made out for Christmas cards than for presents. Everyone you can think of, including many people you've met only once in your life, gets one. And you yourself receive dozens of appalling cards from every business firm and trader you have ever dealt with. Your garage sends you one, so does your TV dealer and your fish-monger and anyone else who thinks you may spend money with him during the coming year. There is nothing more irritating than a Christmas card signed Anne, John or Jane. "Why don't people put their surnames?" I invariably cry as the pile gets higher and higher.

Surely the worst racket of all is the charity Christmas card business. I know a bit about this because in 1989 Quentin Blake and I did a charity card. Had it not been for the help given to us by Penguin Books and others, very little money would have been raised. But Penguin persuaded the paper-makers, the envelope manufacturers, the printers and several other generous firms in the manufacturing chain to give everything free. Even then the cards wouldn't have sold if we had not allowed the booksellers to take their 30 or 40 percent cut of the retail price. I am not telling you to ignore charity cards. They are better than non-charity ones. But you should be aware that, with the exception of a very few who make special arrangements, only a minute percentage of the price you pay finds its way to the charity itself. In many cases the people who make them and sell them to you take most of it.

Then you have the office parties, appalling drunken orgies at which the senior men, stupified by drink and dribbling from the mouth, descend upon typists who they wouldn't deign to speak to during the rest of the year. The orgies are more common than you imagine and it's all part of the great Christian festival of Christmas.

And then comes the ritual of the turkey. It used always to be a goose (which tastes wondeful) or a plump capon, but some time ago someone decided that turkey was the thing to serve for Christmas dinner. Turkey breeders proliferated and millions of these birds were bred and fed in long sheds that kept their flourescent lights on day and night to force the turkeys into gorging themselves round the clock. The breeders make a packet, as did the retailers, and soon virtually every family in Britain was stuffing itself at Christmas on one of the most tasteless meats that it is possible to find. I don't know quite what is drier and more flavorless than a roast turkey. Its only virtue seems to be that one bird goes a long way—so long, in fact, that the family is usually eating it cold or hashed up for the next week.

No, I don't like Christmas and always feel rather as though I have come through a long and fearful battle when it is over. Give it to the children by all means, but do not spoil them with overexpensive presents. Let all of us adults try to make it fun for the children, too, but heaven preserve us from trying to whip up false jollity among ourselves. Christmas used to be a wonderful and dignified Christian occasion. It is now the most important money-making period in the manufacturing industry.

—ROALD DAHL
Memories with Food

A True Bill Agaynst Christmasse

I will not hear of Christmasse Cheer
   Nor Christmasse Bells a-ringing!
A Christmasse Tree I loathe to see,
   I'm deaf to Carol-singing.

I will not troll ye Wassail Bowl!
   I love no strong Potations,
Nor Yule that brings ye Gatherings
   Of Nondescript Relations.

Forebeare to show ye Mistletoe!
   All Proper Men disdain it;
Ye Prettie Maid wolde scorn its Aid,
   Ye Plaine One sholde not gain it.

Give Pause, give Pause to Santa Claus!
   His Course is trulie shocking;
I understand he has a Hande
   In Everybodie's Stocking!

Yet, void of Shame, they praise his Name
   In Reams of idle Verses,
And call him kind that leaves behind
   A Trail of emptie Purses.

Sharp Sorrows lie in Christmasse Pie
   Which treble when they heat it.

I have no Use for Christmasse Goose
  Nor Cannibals that eat it.

For Ills and Pills and Doctor's Bills
  Are scarce a Cause for Laughter;
Ye Tables groan before ye Feaste,
  Ye Feasters groan thereafter.

—ARTHUR GUITERMAN

Lines for Twelfth Night
(As the Holiday Party Season Ends)

I swing between wishing that I were dead
And thinking that maybe I am.

—PYKE JOHNSON, JR.

Early in life I developed a distaste for the Cratchits that time has not sweetened. I do not think I was an embittered child, but the Cratchits' aggressive worthiness, their bravely borne poverty, their exultation over that wretched goose, disgusted me. I particularly disliked Tiny Tim . . . and when he chirped "God bless us, every one!" my mental response was akin to Sam Goldwyn's famous phrase, "Include me out."

—ROBERTSON DAVIES

There are some people who want to throw their arms around you simply because it is Christmas; there are other people who want to strangle you simply because it is Christmas.

—ROBERT LYND

I could never see why people were so happy about Dickens' *A Christmas Carol* because I never had any confidence that Scrooge was going to be different the next day.

—DR. KARL MENNINGER
A Psychiatrist's World

Christmas comes, but once a year is enough.

—ANONYMOUS

The problem with Christmas—rather like having a baby—is that it occurs infrequently enough for us to be able each time to blot out the horrors of the previous one.

—JILLY COOPER

In the United States Christmas has become the rape of an idea.

—RICHARD BACH
Jonathan Livingston Seagull

How many observe Christ's birthday! How few, his precepts! O! 'tis easier to keep holidays than commandments.

—BENJAMIN FRANKLIN
Poor Richard's Almanack

Christmas is only for servants.

—EMERALD CUNARD

Or consider Christmas—could Satan in his most malignant mood have devised a worse combination of graft plus buncombe than the system whereby several hundred million people get a billion or so gifts for which they have no use, and some thousands of shop-clerks die of exhaustion while selling them, and every other child in the western world is made ill from over-eating—all in the name of the lowly Jesus?

—UPTON SINCLAIR
Money Writes!

I am sorry to have to introduce the subject of Christmas. . . . It is an indecent subject; a cruel, gluttonous subject; a drunken, disorderly subject; a wasteful disastrous subject; a wicked, cadging, lying, filthy, blasphemous, and demoralizing subject. Christmas is forced on a reluctant and disgusted nation by the shopkeepers and the press: on its own merits it would wither and shrivel in the fiery breath of universal hatred; and anyone who looked back to it would be turned into a pillar of greasy sausages.

—GEORGE BERNARD SHAW
Our Theatres in the Nineties

Something in me resists the calendar expectation of happiness. *Merry Christmas yourself!* it mutters as it shapes a ghostly grin.

—J. B. PRIESTLEY
Outcries and Asides

Christmas is a holiday that persecutes the lonely, the frayed, and the rejected.

—JIMMY CANNON

When the

Year

Comes to a

Head

Not only does the entire country grind to a halt for a fortnight over the actual holiday, but Christmas starts in the shops in September, so that by the time you get to 25 December you're absolutely fed up to the walnut-filled cavities with the whole thing.

—JILLY COOPER

Overrated disturbances of routine, costly and uncomfortable, and . . . in need of another holiday to correct the ravages.

—EDWARD LUCAS

Nothing satisfies us on Christmas Eve but to hear each other tell authentic anecdotes about specters. It is a genial, festive season, and we love to muse upon graves, and dead bodies, and murder.

—JEROME K. JEROME
Told After Supper

I think that I shall never be
Sold on an artificial tree,

A Christmas tree with plastic limbs
Just doesn't stir me up to hymns;
A tree with needles made of foil,
That grew in factories, not soil;
And, though it will not burn or shed,
Will neither be alive or dead.
Perennial, yes, it may be,
And formed in perfect symmetry.
But only God can make a tree
To suit old-fashioned guys like me.

—ANONYMOUS

Scrooge in a Manger

Once in his childhood he'd heard angels sing
and seen them moving in the aurora borealis
but that was before Muzak made
hearing them impossible,* and before
somebody in Bloomington, Illinois
who still liked Christmas enough to

*John Gardner, *October Light* (Knopf, 1976), p. 13

dress up in red and hand out leaflets
telling shoppers to go home and
celebrate it right, was
arrested for criminal trespassing.**
Yesterday when he went down to the shopping
    center
he observed the decor at the drive-in bank:
oversize fake holly, fake white poinsettias,
fake evergreens both gilded and ungilded,
styrofoam bells tied up in ersatz red velvet
and comes from an honest-to-God pine
tree.***

—AMY CLAMPITT

What's Your Christmas I.2.?

Now is that time of year when our hearts and minds
turn toward joyous thoughts of making other people
happy. But each year it gets a bit more difficult to keep
our own spirits up. Do you possess true Christmas joy,
or are you merely going through the motions? Your

**The New York Times, December 23, 1977
***Personal observation

answers to the following questions may help you to determine your own relationship to the holiday—i.e., are you a Scrooge? Or are you a benevolent, idealistic purveyor of Christmas cheer? Do you truly love Christmas? No sense fooling yourself and your loved ones any longer. Let's get down to business.

Answer each question as truthfully as possible; then turn to page 23 to tally your score. And blessings on us everyone!

1. Which Santa do you truly believe in?

   a. Santa Claus
   b. Santa Barbara
   c. Santa Anita

2. When you send out Christmas cards each year, you

   a. send them c.o.d.
   b. sign every one.
   c. sign every one and add a personal message.
   d. include a two-page photocopied newsletter telling every intimate thing that has happened to you and your family during the year. *(If you do not send out Christmas cards, there is no reason for you to continue with this quiz. You have already shown a lack of the proper Christmas spirit and therefore have flunked. Hey—do you think we're just fooling around here?)*

3. On Christmas Day (usually December 25) where would you prefer to be?

a. Aruba
b. The North Pole

4. What three little words do you feel best sum up for you the spirit of Christmas?

a. I love you.
b. Let's return it.

5. Pretend that today is May 1. How many shopping days are there until Christmas?

a. 203
b. Not enough

6. Your idea of the perfect Christmas dinner is:

a. reindeer.
b. any food you do not have to prepare yourself or clean up.

7. Upon which day of the week will Christmas fall in 1996?

a. Monday
b. Tuesday
c. Wednesday
d. All of the above

8. Which proverb do you feel is most applicable to the Christmas season?

a. "It is better to give than to receive."
b. "A fool and his money are soon parted."

9. Which book is your favorite to read aloud at Christmastime?

　　a. A Christmas Carol
　　b. How to Avoid Probate

10. You forgot to send a Christmas card to your boss. How do you feel?

　　a. Guilty
　　b. Ashamed
　　c. Afraid
　　d. Smug

11. When a 5-year-old child, in tears, runs up to you and asks, "Is there really such a person as Santa Claus?" you answer:

　　a. "Of course there is a Santa Claus. He lives in all our hearts."
　　b. "Drop dead, you little twit."

12. How much money (in U.S. dollars) did you spend for a Christmas tree last year?

　　a. $400, for a four-foot tree
　　b. Less than $400
　　c. Zero

(If you did not put up a Christmas tree, or if you use the same artificial tree year after year, deduct 100 points from your total score.)

13. Who were the Three Wise Men?

a. Larry, Moe and Curly
b. Tinkers to Evers to Chance
c. The Kingston Trio
d. Gaspar, Melchior, Balthazar

14. When filling Christmas stockings for children, which kind of fruit do you usually place into the toe?

a. An orange
b. Prunes

15. Which of the following is not the name of one of Santa's reindeer?

a. Madonna
b. Grumpy
c. Dopey
d. Gorbachev
e. All of the above

16. Which of the sentences below best sums up your feelings?

a. Christmas is too religious.
b. Christmas is too commercial.
c. All of the above

17. During which month of the year do you feel it is most appropriate for merchants to begin placing Christmas decorations in their stores?

a. June
b. July

c. August

d. November, but not until after Thanksgiving

18. Which mode of transportation most reminds you of Christmas?

a. A sleigh

b. The Concorde

c. The *Titanic*

19. Which of the following biblical verses do you feel best sums up the holiday season?

a. "Jesus wept"

b. "And it came to pass"

20. On Christmas morning, which gift would you prefer to get from your own true love?

a. Ten lords a-leaping

b. Eight maids a-milking

c. A partridge in a pear tree

d. A gold bracelet

e. A copy of the swimsuit issue of *American Scholar*

21. The final words that St. Nick shouts at the conclusion to "A Visit from Saint Nicholas" are:

a. "Happy Christmas to all, and to all a goodnight."

b. "How sharper than a serpent's tooth it is to have a thankless child!"

BONUS

If you can recite "A Visit from Saint Nicholas" from memory, add 36 points to your total score.

SCORING

1. If you selected **a**, give yourself 25 points. If you selected **b**, or **c**, you get no points. If you live in Santa Barbara or near Santa Anita, subtract 8. What kind of authentic Christmas spirit can you have in California anyway?

2. If you selected **a**, subtract 25. If you selected **b**, add 10. If you selected **c**, add 15. If you selected **d**, subtract 50. Who wants to know that your kids got braces? If you have ever tried using Christmas Seals in place of regulation United States postage on your cards, skip this question altogether.

3. If you selected **a**, subtract 25. If you selected **b**, subtract 100 for lying.

4. Five points for either answer. Where loud neckties are concerned, we refuse to make value judgments.

5. Twenty points for either answer since both are correct.

6. If you selected **a**, subtract 25. If you selected **b**, give yourself 50 points. However, if you spend Christmas Day cooking for your extended family and all your friends, give yourself an added bonus of 100 points.

7. The correct answer is **all of the above** (25 points). By 1996, in order to spur economic growth, Christmas will be celebrated three times a year. If you actually know, without consulting a calendar, what day Christmas is going to fall on in 1996, subtract 75 points for being overzealous.

8. If you selected **a,** give yourself 50 points. If you selected **b,** find yourself an investment counselor.

9. If you selected **a,** subtract 15 points for being too traditional. If you selected **b,** subtract 15 points for not being traditional enough. (Christmastime does bring out contradictory feelings, doesn't it?)

10. Give yourself 5 points. Your feelings are your feelings, and we have no idea what kind of boss you work for. If, on the other hand, you sent a Christmas card and a gift to your boss, subtract 10 points for overdoing things.

11. If you selected **a,** give yourself 200 points. If you selected **b,** then you have no business taking a quiz such as this one. You should be understudying the part of Scrooge.

12. If you selected **a,** give yourself 87 points. If you selected **b,** give yourself 1 point. If you still have last year's tree standing in your living room (let's face it, trees are too expensive to toss out), give yourself an additional 60 points.

13. If you selected **d,** give yourself 35 points. Welcome to the world of Christmas scholarship. You should be praised for your knowledge of the Bible (or Amahl and the Night Visitors, as the case may be).

14. If you selected **a,** give yourself 7 points. If you

selected **b,** give yourself 0 points. If you ever put coals and switches into any child's stockings or wooden shoe, you have already flunked this quiz.

15. The wording of the question is confusing, so give yourself 38 points. Madonna may or may not be one of Santa's reindeer at sometime in the near future. She's capable of anything.

16. If you selected **a,** give yourself 10 points. If you selected **b,** give yourself 5 points. If you selected **c,** subtract 90 points for not being able to make up your mind. The only way to survive Christmas is to be decisive.

17. If you get upset when you see merchants putting out their decorations too early, subtract 80 points from your score. You have more important things to worry about.

18. No points if you chose **a**—Christmas requires more imagination than that! Give yourself 25 points for **b**—the Concorde is clearly the only way Santa could actually complete his rounds. Subtract 10 points for **c,** and talk to your doctor about an antidepressant.

19. If you selected **a,** subtract 10 points. If you selected **b,** give yourself 10 points. Although a desire to see Christmas come and go quickly is in questionable holiday spirit, the quote *does* come from the Nativity story.

20. Ten lords a-leaping is definitely the best choice: 10 points. If you selected the gold bracelet, subtract 12 points. Think big!

21. If you selected **a,** give yourself 20 points. If you selected **b,** give yourself 200 points because you deserve something for having read *King Lear*.

TOTAL YOUR SCORE

If you have scored more than 500 points, you definitely love Christmas. Santa Claus has nothing on you. God bless you every one!

If, on the other hand, you scored less than 500 points, you did at least take the time to ponder the quiz. That proves something about your care and concern, doesn't it? Besides, as far as we know, Christmas will be with us next year. Thus, you have plenty of time to improve your rating.

Bah, humbug! to you too!

—LOUIS PHILLIPS

Roses are reddish,
Violets are bluish.
If it weren't for Xmas
We'd all be Jewish.

—GRAFFITO

A Fragment from a Mummer's Play

Here come I, old Father Christmas,
Come to work you grief and woe,
Come to fill the air with rubbish
On my Bumper Christmas Show.

Rock musicians singing carols,
Celebrities in paper hats,
Politicians being jolly,
Republicans and Democrats.

Now's the time for Family Parties,
Jolly uncles making jokes,
Aunts and cousins by the dozens,
Such hearty eaters, just plain folks.

Now farewell to Father Christmas,
I'll be back another year,
Never mind the winter weather,
It is me you have to fear.

—JOHN SWEETMAN

The

Atrocity

Beneath

the

Wrapper

Whatever the atrocity beneath the wrapper, my smile will be as warm as the devil's hob. "Ah, you shouldn'a," I will shriek, even as I wonder if the wretched thing is combustible, because I know that the gifts I receive are, for awfulness, not a patch on those I give.

—HUGH LEONARD

What He Deserved

A letter that gave Santa pause
Went as follows: HIYA, CLAUS!
I BEEN GOOD, SO GIMME GIMME
LOTS OF TOYS. YOUR OLD PAL, JIMMY.

Santa left that greedy kid
Something that a reindeer did.

—X. J. KENNEDY

The Nightmare Before Christmas

How seldom does the spirit lift
While brooding on the proper gift

For every name that's hieroglyphed
    Upon your list for Noel.
Last year you scarved and handkerchiefed
Your friends and found that present thrift
Produced unpleasant future rift—
    How beastly is bestowal!

What can one give a girl like *her*
Who's said to be a connoisseur
Of emeralds and blended fur?
    It makes you, you confide, sick.
And as for *him*? No easier:
He likes champagne and fine liqueur.
You want to snarl, "Confound the cur!
    Who pays the Piper Heidsieck?"

Instead, you plumb your dwindling hoard
And pray for friends you can afford.

—FELICIA LAMPORT
Cultural Slag

Toying with Toys

Our children get toys from friends,
They get them from relatives too,

And many are toys that break—
We mend them with tape and glue.

Our children get toys for Christmas,
For birthdays, for any old time.
The generous givers are many,
And all I would thank in rhyme.

Our children get toys they scatter,
At finding odd places they're clever,
The givers of toys pick them *out,*
But we pick them *up,* however.

—RICHARD ARMOUR
The Spouse in the House

A Father's Christmas Thought

I'd rather be a pagan, suckled in a creed outworn,
Than face the pandemonium of early Christmas morn.

—WILLIAM COLE

A Thought

I love the Christmas tide, and yet
I notice this, each year I live;
I always like the gifts I get,
But how I love the gifts I give!

—CAROLYN WELLS

Xmas Time

A lonely little girl
Went calmly off to bed
And all the Xmas that she had
Was in her little head.

—WALTA KARSNER
(Written at age nine)

Last Christmas I bought a hobby horse for my grand-daughter. It came in a large box which said it contained 189 parts and could be put together in one hour. Sure it could, if you've just graduated from MIT and have a machine shop in your basement. I didn't have to accept that kind of indignity, so, when I went to pay for it, I tore my check in 189 pieces and wrote them a little note telling them if they like to put things together let them work on that. One sad ending to my story . . . they did!

—BILL VEECK

The first rule in buying Christmas presents is to select something shiny. If the chosen object is of leather, the leather must look as if it had been well greased; if of silver, it must gleam with the light that never was on sea or land. This is because the wariest person will often mistake shininess for expensiveness.

—P. G. WODEHOUSE
Louder and Funnier

I love Christmas. I receive a lot of wonderful presents I can't wait to exchange.

—HENNY YOUNGMAN

Ever since Eve gave Adam the apple, there has been a misunderstanding between the sexes about gifts.

—NAN ROBERTSON
New York Times

Christmas is a widely observed holiday on which neither the past nor the future is of so much interest as the present.

—F. G. KERNAN

You never git what you want fer Christmus after you grow up.

—KIN HUBBARD
"Abe Martin"

I find it difficult to believe in Father Christmas. If he is the jolly old gentleman he is always said to be, why doesn't he behave as such? How is it that the presents go so often to the wrong people?

—A. A. MILNE
Not That It Matters

Gifts are like fish-hooks.

—MARTIAL

A gift long waited for is sold, not given.

—AMERICAN PROVERB

One of the first things a boy who gets a drum set for Christmas learns is that he isn't likely to ever get another one.

—ANONYMOUS

Our children await Christmas presents like politicians getting election returns; there's the Uncle Fred precinct and the Aunt Ruth district still to come in.

—MARCELENE COX
Ladies Home Journal

How painful to give a gift to any person of sensibility, or of equality! It is next worst to receiving one.

—RALPH WALDO EMERSON
Essays: Second Series

Everybody knows that everybody gives everybody else bath essence, or bath salts, or bath powder for Christmas.

—*VIRGINIA GRAHAM*
Everything's Too Something

So much, indeed, is there to be said for and against any view about giving presents, that it is safer not to think about it, but to buy your presents first, and afterwards to consider what, if anything, you will do with them. After all, if you decide in the end not to give them to anyone, you can always keep them.

—*ROSE MACAULAY*
A Casual Commentary

The way in which Father Christmas's sack is overloaded clearly contravenes all the safety regulations for the carriage of goods by air.

—*LORD MANCROFT*
A Chinaman in My Bath

A woman who is insidiously ostentatious about the flowerlike and impersonal quality of her beauty can be given a hot-water bottle or small biscuit-colored Shetland shawl to wear in bed or a tin of patent food which announces clearly on the front label that it has been specially treated to make it more easily digestible. . . . Thrown in with the rest somebody can give her a cheap lipstick, smelling of lard.

—STEPHEN POTTER
One-Upmanship

A jolly little poker-work doggie which pops in and out of a kennel shaped like a shoe is a splendid present to give to either (a) a zoologist, (b) a collector of Staffordshire glaze, or (c) a breeder of pedigree poodles. To one's wife, of course, one gives the present one wants oneself—a book on astronomy, for instance, or even one on golf, "in the hope that she will really start to play, now."

—STEPHEN POTTER
Supermanship

Why It Is So Difficult to Give an Elephant as Gift for Christmas

Of all the facts I know,
This is most relevant:
It takes a lot of paper
To gift-wrap an elephant.

—LOUIS PHILLIPS

Mock Christmas Carol

Jesus Christ was born today!
Hooray, hooray, hooray, hooray!
Whatever any of you may say
He was born to cancel our terrible sins
And save us all from loony bins!
Hooray, hooray, hooray!

Jesus Christ was born today!
Hooray, hooray, hooray, hooray!

This is no time to watch and pray,
Let's all get drunk and drink a toast
To the Virgin Mary and the Holy Ghost!
Hooray, hooray, hooray!

Jesus Christ was born today!
Hooray, hooray, hooray, hooray!
Over-eating's a lovely way
To do Him honor; each Yuletide gift
Gives Him a God Almighty lift!
Hooray, hooray, hooray!

—*GAVIN EWART*
Collected Poems 1980–1990

"I'm Dreaming of a White Christmas"

With another Christmas at our throats in a mere ten days, the problem I confront is one that's been cropping up more and more these past few years. I've found out what I'm going to be given—and I don't want it.

I mention this predicament because I believe that somewhere within it lies the answer to the frequently asked question, "What's gone wrong with the English Christmas?" To my mind, the deterioration dates back to whenever it was people stopped buying each other presents and began buying each other gifts.

Because there is a very real difference. A present is something given in the hope that it will fulfil a need or expectation. Gifts are things you buy from Gift Shops.

No High Street today is complete without its Gift Shop, usually standing where late there was a small bakery, or a cobbler's (how *did* the word for those eminently valuable tradesmen decline into its present expletive application?), or an ironmonger's where you could get a key cut while you waited, or a fruiterer who stayed open till midnight, or a drapers where the old lady would cash a check for you. A Gift Shop is staffed by a man who wears a brown suede jacket and puts the word "only" in front of every price ("Only £386"). Its heavily tarted-up front window displays a small figurine of a shepherdess with a clock in her navel, magnetized backgammon boards, Moroccan drink-trays that have nothing to lift them up by, and things known as Executive Toys: these are designed to sit on a broad expanse of empty desk and either hit one part of themselves against another part, or flash a succession of tiny lights in so random a fashion that you begin to realize why so many stockbrokers are jumping out of windows.

Those are gifts, as distinct from presents. They are the new "giving-objects," artifacts designed not for use or enjoyment but simply as currency for Christmas transactions. Within the shop's bedizened interior you can purchase loo-seats that shine in the dark, Mickey Mouse sundials, cans of spray-on dandruff, battery-operated toothpicks, polythene snowmen and a frozen mushroom-pizza with "Happy Xmas" spelt out in anchovies.

And, of all these non-felt wants, the one that makes my heart sink almost to knee-level is the gift for which, so I've discovered, my well-meaning sister paid out her good money this Yuletide—a Scandinavian Candle-Making Kit. The cinema in my skull is already screening its presentation ceremony: "Oh, it's a candle-making kit! . . . And *Scandinavian!*"

"You sure you haven't got one?"

"I'm practically certain."

Are you familiar with that particular kind of jaw-muscle ache that comes only from maintaining a grateful smile for six hours? The kind where you become convinced you're going to have to send for a doctor because your face has locked? I'll be down with it practically all Christmas Day. And I can also tell you the moment I fear most.

"Aren't you going to try it? Oh, go on. Make a candle for Auntie Rose."

My handedness at all manual endeavors is so invincibly cack, I can hardly bear thinking about all those lumps of wax and rolls of wick and plastic molds—and *hot tallow!*

If any of you are curious to know which seasonal tune I'll be caroling Christmas Day after the relatives have departed, I can already hum it for you:

"I'm cleaning off a white grease mess."

—DENIS NORDEN

The Twelve Days of Christmas

December 14
Dear John:

I went to the door today and the postman delivered a partridge in a pear tree. What a thoroughly delightful gift. I couldn't have been more surprised.

With deepest love and devotion, Agnes

December 15
Dearest John:

Today the postman brought your very sweet gift. Just imagine . . . two turtle doves. I'm just delighted at your very thoughtful gift. They are just adorable.

All my love, Agnes

December 16
Dear John:

Oh! Aren't you the extravagant one. Now I must really protest. I don't deserve such generosity . . . three French hens! They are just darling but I must insist, you've been too kind.

Love, Agnes

December 17
Dear John:

Today the postman delivered four calling birds.

Now really, they are beautiful, but don't you think enough is enough? You're being too romantic.

Affectionately, Agnes

December 18
Dearest John:

What a surprise. Today the postman delivered five golden rings, one for every finger. You're just impossible, but I love it. Frankly, all those birds squawking were beginning to get on my nerves.

All my love, Agnes.

December 19
Dear John:

I opened my door today and there were actually six geese alaying on my front steps. So you're back to the birds again, huh? These geese are huge! Where will I keep them? The neighbors are complaining and I can't sleep through this racket!

Please stop.

Cordially, Agnes

December 20
Dear John:

What's with you and these **** birds? Seven swans a-swimming! What kind of goddam joke is this? There's bird **** all over the house and they never stop with the racket. I can't sleep at night and I'm a nervous wreck. It's not funny so stop with those **** birds.

Sincerely, Agnes

December 21

OK, buster . . . I think I prefer the birds. What the hell am I going to do with eight maids a-milking? It's not enough with all those birds and the maids, but they brought their damn cows. Lay off me, smartass!

Agnes

December 22

Hey, ****-head! What are you some kind of sadist? Now there's nine pipers playing! And Christ, do they play. They never stopped chasing those maids since they got here. The cows are upset and they're stepping all over the birds, and the neighbors have started a petition to evict me!

You'll get yours, Agnes

December 23

You rotten ****. Now there's ten ladies dancing! I don't know why I call those sluts ladies. They've been balling those pipers all night long. Now the cows can't sleep and they've got diarrhea. The commissioner of buildings has subpoenaed me to give cause why the building shouldn't be condemned. I'm siccing the police on you!

One who means it.

December 24

Listen ****-head, what's with the eleven lords a-leaping on those maids and ladies? Some of those broads will never walk again! The pipers ran through all the maids and have been committing sodomy with the cows. All twenty-three birds are dead. They got trampled in the orgy. I hope you're satisfied, you rotten vicious swine!

Your sworn enemy, Agnes

December 25
Dear Sir:

This is to acknowledge your latest gift of twelve fiddlers fiddling which you have inflicted upon our client Agnes Mendolstein. The destruction was total. All future correspondence should come to our attention. If you should attempt to reach Miss Mendolstein at the Happy Dale Sanitarium, the attendants have instructions to shoot you on sight. Please find attached a warrant for your arrest.

Law Offices
Budger, Bender & Cahole

—ANONYMOUS

Curses on the Cards

One of the curses of Christmas is the Christmas cards with gaudy linings which resemble the inside of a drunkard's stomach.

—DON HEROLD

Don't send any funny greeting cards on birthdays or at Christmas. Save them for funerals, when their cheery effect is needed.

—P. J. O'ROURKE
Modern Manners

In early January friendly Christmas cards continue to arrive, struggling gamely home like the last few stragglers on a London Marthon.

—ARTHUR MARSHALL
Sunny Side Up

I was glad to get a letter instead of a Christmas card.
A Christmas card is a rather innutritious thing.

—OSCAR W. FIRKINS
Memoirs and Letters

Happy Birthday, Jesus!

(Sign near Houston Airport at Christmastime)

Olé, Jesús!

(Sign in Tijuana at Christmastime)

Christmas Greetings for 1923

There was a man in our town
And he was wondrous wise:

He said he'd never send a Christmas
   Card to any guys.

But when he opened up his mail
   From many friends and cousins,
He jumped into a stationer's shop
   And sent out several dozens.

                    —FRANKLIN P. ADAMS
                    So There!

Lines for a Christmas Card

May all my enemies go to hell,
Noël, Noël, Nöel, Nöel.

                    —HILAIRE BELLOC

Lines for a Card

To the fir tree on its slope
Christmas brings no sign of hope.
To the turkey in the yard
Christmas seems a trifle hard.
To the pauper on the street
Christmastide is none too sweet.
But to one who scribbles rhymes,
Christmas is the best of times,
Complete with cliché, fake devotion
and instant access to emotion:
Stable, manger, Joseph, Mary,
(Pass the rhyming dictionary).
To the couple in the stable
Who provide us with the fable
Christmas may have been quite bleak
(Not so the poetic clique).

—GERARD BENSON

The Computer's First Christmas Card

jollymerry
hollyberry
jollyberry
merryholly
happyjolly
jollyjelly
jellybelly
bellymerry
hollyheppy
jollyMolly
marryJerry
merryHarry
hoppyBarry
heppyJarry
boppyheppy
berryjorry
jorryjolly
moppyjelly
Mollymerry
Jerryjolly
bellyboppy
jorryhoppy
hollymoppy

Barrymerry
Jarryhappy
happyboppy
boppyjolly
jollymerry
merrymerry
merrymerry
merryChris
ammerryasa
Chrismerry
asMERRYCHR
YSANTHEMUM

—EDWIN MORGAN
The Second Life

Waiting
for Santy

Hark

Hark! the Christmas bells are ringing,
Gangs of little scruffs are singing
       Carols out of tune.
Traffic jams are snarling, hooting,
There has even been a shooting.
       Christmas comes too soon.
       Ding-dong, bang-bang,
       Vroom-vroom, clang-clang!
       Christmas comes too soon.

Round the crib the kids are kneeling,
Grandma's thumping on the ceiling,
       (Hear the plaster fall).
Mother's drunk and father's swearing,
Aunt Penelope's preparing
       "Drinkies" for us all.
       Thump-thump, slurp-slurp,
       Grunt-grunt, burp-burp!
       Drinkies for us all.

Slush is freezing in the gutter.
"Uncle Jack can't last," they mutter,
       "Hear the way he

coughed?"
Yule is on us. Look at Santa,
Swigging straight from the decanter.
Christmas comes too oft.
Brrr-brrr, clink-clink,
Cough-cough, drink-drink!
Christmas comes too oft.

—GERARD BENSON

No sane local official who has hung up an empty stocking over the municipal fireplace is going to shoot Santa Claus just before a hard Christmas.

—ALFRED E. SMITH
New Outlook, December 1933

I never believed in Santa Claus because I knew no white dude would come into my neighborhood after dark.

—DICK GREGORY

Santa Claus has the right idea; visit people once a year.

—VICTOR BORGE

A cynic is just a man who found out when he was about ten that there wasn't any Santa Claus, and he's still upset.

—JAMES GOULD COZZENS

St. Nick Is Too Thick

Saint Nicholas wiped his brow, and wheezed, "By Jiminy—
I get Santa Claustrophobia in a chiminey!"

—WILLIAM COLE

Santa Claus has arrived: an event that in the past has unfailingly had the same effect on me as a foaming beaker had on Dr. Henry Jekyll.

—HUGH LEONARD
Sunday Independent, Dublin

I stopped believing in Santa Claus when I was six. Mother took me to see him in a department store and he asked for my autograph.

—SHIRLEY TEMPLE

Santa is even-tempered.Santa does not hit children over the head who kick him. Santa uses the term *folks* rather than *Mommy and Daddy* because of all the broken homes. Santa does not have a three-martini lunch. Santa does not borrow money from store employees. Santa wears a good deodorant.

—JENNY ZINK
(To employees of Western Temporary Services,
supplier of department store Santas)

WHAT IS THE DIFFERENCE BETWEEN GOD AND SANTA CLAUS?
ANSWER: THERE IS A SANTA CLAUS.

—GRAFFITO

IF YOU CAN BELIEVE IN TINY TIM, SANTA CLAUS SHOULD BE EASY.

—GRAFFITO

Out There on the Sidewalk

(Sung to the Tune of "Away in a Manger")

Out there on the sidewalk a Santa Claus stands
Beside a fake chimney, a bell in his hands;
A second one's smoking a smelly cigar;
A third one is picking his teeth in a bar.

A fourth Santa's trying to pick up a blonde;
A fifth one is drunk in the gutter beyond;
A sixth one is part of a window display;
The seventh and eighth ones appear to be gay.

They're fat and they're skinny, they're short and
they're tall;
And none looks a bit like the real one at all;
With so many Santas, it's tough to keep
score—
Small wonder that kids don't believe anymore.

—FRANK JACOBS
Mad

The Month Before Christmas
(A Non-Scheduled Visit from St. Nicholas)

'Twas a month before Christmas, and all through
    the store
Each department was dripping with Yuletide decor;
The Muzak was blaring an out-of-tune carol
And fake snow was falling on "Ladies' Apparel."

I'd flown many miles from the North Pole this day
To check on reports that had caused me dismay;
I'd come to this store but for one special reason:
To see for myself what went on at this Season.

I hid in a corner and in a short while
I saw the Store President march down an aisle;
He shouted an order to "Turn the store tree on!"
And also the "NOEL" in blinding pink neon.

Up high, grandly swinging from twin gold supports,
Four hundred pink angels flew over "Men's Shorts,"
And towering over the Rear Mezzanine—
A ninety-foot Day-Glo "Nativity Scene."

The clock on the wall said two minutes to nine;
The floorwalkers proudly all stood in a line;
I watched while the President smelled their
    carnations

Then called out his final command—"Man Your
   Stations!"

When out on the street there arose such a roar!
It rang to the rafters and boomed through the store!
It sounded exactly like street repair drilling—
Or maybe another big Mafia killing.

I looked to the doors, and there banging the glass
Was a clamoring, shrieking, hysterical mass,
And I felt from the tone of each scream and each
   curse
That the "Spirit of Christmas" had changed for the
   worse.

The clock it struck nine and the door opened wide
And that great human avalanche thundered inside:
More fearsome than Sherman attacking Atlanta
Came parents and kiddies with just one goal—
   "Santa!"

In front stormed the mothers, all brandishing
   handbags
As heavy and deadly as twenty-pound sandbags;
With gusto they swung them, the better to smash
   ears
Of innocent floorwalkers, buyers and cashiers.

Straight up to the Fifth Floor the mob penetrated
And soon reached the room where the store Santa
   waited;

I followed them closely, the better to see
This bearded imposter who dared to play me.

He stood six-foot-five and weighed all of 130;
He'd lost half his teeth and his costume was dirty;
His beard dangled down like a wad of cheap cotton;
His breath needed Scope and his "ho-ho" was
        rotten.

Egged on by their parents, the kids had one aim;
To get to this man who was using my name;
They mobbed him and mauled him, the better to
        plead
For the presents they sought in their hour of greed.

The President watched with a gleam in his eye
As he thought of the toys that the parents would
        buy;
Of all Christmas come-ons, this crowd would attest
That a visit to "Santa" was surely the best.

It all was too much for my soul to condone
And I let out a most unprofessional moan;
The crowd turned around, and I'll say for their sake
That they knew in an instant I wasn't a fake,

"I've had it," I told them, "with fast-buck
        promoting,
With gimmicks and come-on and businessmen
        gloating;

This garish display of commercialized greed
Is so very UN-Christmas, it makes my heart bleed!"

With that I departed and, shouting a farewell,
Went barreling up an emergency stairwell;
On reaching the roof, to my sleigh I went forth
Where my reindeer were waiting to take me back
    North.

The crowd swarmed behind me to beg me to stay;
Before they could speak, I was off in my sleigh;
But I turned to exclaim as I flew from the mob—
"Happy Christmas to all—I'm resigning my job!"

                —FRANK JACOBS
                  Mad

The Misanthrope's Christmas

Christmas comes but once a Year—thank God;
If it came twice, we'd think it rather odd:
We'd sit, & curse, & make out those dam' Lists,
And watch them mulitply like canc'rous Cysts.
Ahoy, the blinking Lights—a Constellation!
Punches, & Parties, & ruddy-fac'd Damnation!

What are they merry for? Just tell me that—
Because another's Lean, & they are Fat?
Because their Cheeks with Goose & Stuffing
    wobble,
Because their Weasands like a Turkey's gobble?
Or is it that they, now departing, go,
And leave no bloody Footprint in the Snow?
Enough, I say, of all this glitt'ring Folly,
Enough of Trees, & ever-blooming Holly,
Enough of sugar'd Cards, & candies Saws,
Enough—yes, I will speak—of Santa Claus!
Who, were he hung from yonder Evergreen,
Would make a pleasant Picture, as I ween.
Hang him, & let the World go dark, I say,
And when 'tis Night, do not tell me it's Day.

—JOHN MELLA

A Farewell to Santa Claus
(Or, Violins Are Nice for Boys with Chins)

(The idea of this playlet grew gradually in the mind
of the writer while he was quietly trying to read Chek-

hov's *Notebooks* at a cocktail party where the guests were discussing Hemingway, while one man in a lady's hat was imitating Ed Wynn.)

[*It is Christmas Eve. Santa Claus, in a patched suit, is working on a wooden toy, using only a gouge, for he has had to sell his other tools. In one corner his wife is dying of grief; in another corner a student is attempting suicide. Enter from time to time several Italian army officers and Russian government clerks.*]

SANTA CLAUS: This toy is no good.

JUNIOR CLAUS: I am cold.

MRS. CLAUS: Hush.

STUDENT: What, no prosperity! [*Shoots self.*]

ARMY OFFICER: It's no good flying all over the world with one toy.

SANTA CLAUS: As each child reaches for it, I will pull it back up the chimney. It will teach them they can't even trust Santa Claus.

JUNIOR: I am hungry.

MRS. CLAUS [*rocking back and forth, keening*]: When I was a young woman, I married a prominent myth. I ceased to believe in him and he no longer existed. Then my son believed, and my husband existed again.

JUNIOR: I don't believe in him. [*Santa Claus vanishes.*]

CLERK: I believe in him. [*Santa Claus reappears.*]

SANTA CLAUS: Cut it out. This toy is no good.

MRS. CLAUS: Never make toys, Junior. Make practical

things. Your father will teach you to make practical things.

SANTA CLAUS: I don't know how to make practical things. I know how to make toys.

JUNIOR [*whining*]: I don't want to make toys. I want to make practical things.

SANTA CLAUS: All right, I'll teach you to make practical things, but they're not going to *look* like practical things.

OFFICER: It's going to be a hard winter. It's no good having a hard winter. The reindeer will die of cold.

SANTA CLAUS: The reindeer are no good.

JUNIOR: I want to kill a storekeeper. I want to shoot myself.

CLERK [*moodily, holding up piece of rope*]: I have either lost a horse or am about to hang myself.

MRS. CLAUS: I don't like the rain. I am afraid of the rain.

CLERK: It is no good having rain.

SANTA CLAUS: It is time to go. [*Santa puts on an old hat and an old coat, and puts his one toy in an old bag. He whistles for his reindeer.*]

MRS. CLAUS: I am afraid of the rain.

FIRST REINDEER [*putting nose in doorway*]: I am no good.

MRS. CLAUS: Nothing is any good.

SANTA CLAUS: Which deer are you? You all look so much alike.

REINDEER: I am Vixen. Who are *you?*

SANTA CLAUS: [*aside*]: He doesn't know me. I have grown so thin and emaciated; I am so gaunt and pale. [*to the reindeeer*] You know me. I'm sure you know me. Look. [*He smiles in a pathetic attempt at jollity, tries to shake his sides like a bowl of jelly, blows out his sunken cheeks.*] See? Remember?

[*The reindeer studies him in a puzzled way for a few moments, then brightens slightly, and points a hoof at him.*]

REINDEER: Are you a short, fat man?

[*Outside, sleighbells are ringing and bits of torn-up pencil-tablets, shaded to represent rain, drift by the window.*]

SANTA CLAUS: Well, I'm off. Nothing ever happens to the brave.

[*He swings his bag, with the one toy in it, over his shoulder, whistles with affected cheer, goes over to kiss Mrs. Claus, and finds she has died of grief. He stands looking at her. He doesn't say anything.*]

SANTA CLAUS [*slowly*]: Her word was law. It's like saying goodbye to a statute.

[*He walks to a hotel in the rain.*]

JUNIOR: I'm hungry.

ITALIAN OFFICER: Eat some cheese.

JUNIOR: I don't like cheese. Cheese is for rats.

OFFICER [*angrily*]: Let the rats have it.

[*Machine-gun fire offstage. All fall riddled except one*

government clerk. He hangs himself from the chimney
with a stocking. Not a creature is stirring.]

[CURTAIN]

—JAMES THURBER

Christmas Scene, Dublin

The man with the accordion
Was Father Christmas. Anyone
Would know him by the scarlet dress,
The whiskers, and the portliness.
He looked a proper saint and merry,
Except for the extraordinary
Instrument on which he played
While children listened undismayed
As to a solemn music, sweet
At Christmas, on a Dublin street—

Befitting to the time of year.
In dazzlement they stood to hear
The bursting melody, the one
Air for the accordion
In Father Christmas' repertory.
And as he played it, *con amore*—
His face a mirror of each face
Of small ones of the populace—

He warbled, like a fat canary,
"It's a Long Way to Tipperary."

—HELEN BEVINGTON
A Change of Sky

Naughty Santa

Naughty, naughty Santa. Like a melon overripe,
He's clinically obese—and always puffing on that
    pipe.
His rubicund complexion says his pressure's pushing
    highs
And only once a year does he engage in exercise.
And as for his cholesterol, on Christmas Eve it
    zooms,
A consequence of all the milk and cookies he
    consumes.
He lifts his heavy burdens with nobody to assist.
(Of all that Santa gives us, bad example heads the
    list.)

—BOB McKENTY

Nothingmas Day

Lots o' Christmusses have been ruined by not carvin'
the turkey in th' kitchen.

—KIN HUBBARD
"Abe Martin"

Christmas Family Reunion

Since last the tutelary hearth
    Has seen the bursting pod of kin,
I've thought how good the family mould,
    How solid and how genuine.

Now once again the aunts are here,
    The uncles, sisters, brothers,
With candy in the children's hair,
    The grownups in each other's.

There's talk of saving room for pie;
    Grandma discusses her neuralgia.
I long for time to pass, so I
    Can think of all this with nostalgia.

—PETER DeVRIES
The Tents of Wickedness

April Yule, Daddy!

Roses are things which Christmas is not a bed of
    them,
Because it is the day when parents finally realize that
    their children will alway be a jump ahead of
    them.
You stay up all night trimming the tree into a
    veritable fairyland and then in the joyous morn
    you spring it on the children in a blaze of
    glory, and who says Ooh!?

You.
And you frantically point out the dictator's ransom
    in building sets and bicycles and embarrassingly
    lifelike dolls with which the room is checkered,
And the little ones pay about as much attention to
    them as they would to the punctuation in the
    Congressional Record,
Because they are fully occupied in withdrawing all
    the books from the bookcase to build a house
    to house the pup in,
Or pulling down the curtains to dress up in,
And you stand hangdoggedly around because you
    haven't any place to go,
And after a while they look casually over at the

dictator's ransom and say, "Are those the
presents? Oh."
And you console yourself by thinking Ah happy
apathy, as long as we haven't had an emotional
climax maybe we won't have an emotional
anticlimax, maybe we'll get through the day
without hysterics, ah happy apathy.
Ah may this Yuletide indeed turn out to be Yuletide
without mishapathy.
Ah could this sensational lull but be permanent
instead of pro tem;
Ah and doubly ah, if Christmas day could but end
at eleven A.M.!—
But it doesn't, but the lull does, and here's
something else you discover as you keep on
living,
Which is that Christmas doesn't end for about two
weeks after Christmas, but it starts all over
again right after the following Thanksgiving.

—OGDEN NASH
Verses from 1929 On

A Fresh Brat

To sabotage the Yuletide play
Jealous would-be actor Jay,
Crouching in the prompter's cage
Rolls steel marbles out on stage.

Shepherds slip and somersault,
Shouting, "Nuts! It's not my fault!"—
One crash-lands on Jay. At last
Someone's put him in a cast.

—X. J. KENNEDY
Fresh Brats

Waste

Our governess—would you believe
It? drowned herself on Christmas Eve!
This was a waste, as, anyway,
It would have been a holiday.

—HARRY GRAHAM
When Grandma Fell Off the Boat

A Christmas Letter

(In Answer to a Young Lady Who Has Sent an Invitation to Be Present at a Children's Party)

MADEMOISELLE,

Allow me very gratefully but firmly to refuse your kind invitation. You doubtless mean well; but your ideas are unhappily mistaken.

Let us understand one another once and for all. I cannot at my mature age participate in the sports of children with such abandon as I could wish. I entertain, and have always entertained, the sincerest regard for such games as Hunt-the-Slipper and Blind-Man's Buff. But I have now reached a time of life, when, to have my eyes blindfolded and to have a powerful boy of ten hit me in the back with a hobby-horse and ask me to guess who hit me, provokes me to a fit of retaliation which could only culminate in reckless criminality. Nor can I cover my shoulders with a drawing-room rug and crawl round on my hands and knees under the pretense that I am a bear without a sense of personal insufficiency, which is painful to me.

Neither can I look on with a complacent eye at the sad spectacle of your young clerical friend, the Reverend Mr. Uttermost Farthing, abandoning himself to such gambols and appearing in the role of life and soul of the evening. Such a degradation of his holy calling grieves me, and I cannot but suspect him of ulterior motives.

You inform me that your maiden aunt intends to help you to entertain the party. I have not, as you know, the honor of your aunt's acquaintance, yet I think I may with reason surmise that she will organize games—guessing games—in which she will ask me to name a river in Asia beginning with a Z; on my failure to do so she will put a hot plate down my neck as a forfeit, and the children will clap their hands. These games, my dear young friend, involve the use of a more adaptable intellect than mine, and I cannot consent to be a party to them.

May I say in conclusion that I do not consider a five-cent pen-wiper from the top branch of a Xmas tree any adequate compensation for the kind of evening you propose.

I have the honor
       To subscribe myself,
            Your obedient servant.

                —STEPHEN LEACOCK
                Literary Lapses

A Christmas Spectacle

(For Use in Christmas Eve Entertainments in the Vestry)

At the opening of the entertainment the Superintendent will step into the footlights, recover his balance apologetically, and say:

"Boys and girls of the Intermediate Department, parents and friends: I suppose you all know why we are here to-night. (At this point the audience will titter apprehensively.) Mrs. Drury and her class of little girls have been working very hard to make this entertainment a success, and I am sure that every one here tonight is going to have what I overheard one of my boys the other day calling 'some good time.' (Indulgent laughter from the little boys.) And may I add before the curtain goes up that immediately after the entertainment we want you all to file out into the Christian Endeavour room, where there will be a Christmas tree, 'with all the fixin's,' as the boys say." (Shrill whistling from the boys and immoderate applause from every one.)

There will then be a wait of twenty-five minutes, while sounds of hammering and dropping may be heard from behind the curtains. The Boys' Club orchestra will render the "Poet and Peasant Overture" four times in succession, each time differently.

At last one side of the curtains will be drawn back; the other will catch on something and have to be released by hand; some one will whisper loudly, "Put out the lights," following which the entire house will be plunged into darkness. Amid catcalls from the little boys, the footlights will at last go on, disclosing:

The windows in the rear of the vestry rather ineffectively concealed by a group of small fir trees on standards, one of which has already fallen over, leaving exposed a corner of the map of Palestine and the list of gold-star classes for November. In the center of the stage is a larger tree, undecorated, while at the extreme left, invisible to every one in the audience except those sitting at the extreme right, is an imitation fireplace, leaning against the wall.

Twenty-five seconds too early little Flora Rochester will prance out from the wings, uttering the first shrill notes of a song, and will have to be grabbed by eager hands and pulled back. Twenty-four seconds later the piano will begin "The Return of the Reindeer" with a powerful accent on the first note of each bar, and Flora Rochester, Lillian McNulty, Gertrude Hamingham and Martha Wrist will swirl on, dressed in white, and advance heavily into the footlights, which will go out.

There will then be an interlude while Mr. Neff, the sexton, adjusts the connection, during which the four little girls stand undecided whether to brave it out or cry. As a compromise they giggle and are herded back into the wings by Mrs. Drury, amid applause. When the lights go on again, the applause becomes deafening, and as Mr. Neff walks triumphantly away, the little boys in the audience will whistle: "There she goes, there she goes, all dressed up in her Sunday clothes!"

"The Return of the Reindeer" will be started again and the show-girls will reappear, this time more gingerly and somewhat dispirited. They will, however, sing the following to the music of the "Ballet Pizzicato" from "Sylvia":

> "We greet you, we greet you,
> On this Christmas Eve so fine.
> We greet you, we greet you,
> And wish you a good time."

They will then turn toward the tree and Flora Rochester will advance, hanging a silver star on one of the branches, meanwhile reciting a verse, the only distinguishable words of which are: *"I am Faith so strong and pure —"*

At the conclusion of her recitation, the star will fall off.

Lillian McNulty will then step forward and hang her star on a branch, reading her lines in clear tones:

"And I am Hope, a virtue great,
My gift to Christmas now I make,
That children and grown-ups may hope to-day
That to-morrow will be a merry Christmas Day."

The hanging of the third star will be consummated by Gertrude Hammingham, who will get as far as *"Sweet Charity I bring to place upon the tree—"* at which point the strain will become too great and she will forget the remainder. After several frantic glances toward the wings, from which Mrs. Drury is sending out whispered messages to the effect that the next line begins, *"My message bright—"* Gertrude will disappear, crying softly.

After the morale of the cast has been in some measure restored by the pianist, who, with great presence of mind, plays a few bars of "Will There Be Any Stars In My Crown?" to cover up Gertrude's exit, Martha Wrist will unleash a rope of silver tinsel from the foot of the tree, and, stringing it over the boughs as she skips around in a circle, will say, with great assurance:

> " 'Round and 'round the tree I go,
> Through the holly and the snow
> Bringing love and Christmas cheer
> Through the happy year to come."

At this point there will be a great commotion and jangling of sleigh-bells off-stage, and Mr. Creamer, rather poorly disguised as Santa Claus, will emerge from the opening in the imitation fireplace. A great popular demonstration for Mr. Creamer will follow. He will then advance to the footlights, and, rubbing his pillow and ducking his knees to denote joviality, will say thickly through his false beard:

"Well, well, well, what have we here? A lot of bad little boys and girls who aren't going to get any Christmas presents this year? (Nervous laughter from the little boys and girls.) Let me see, let me see! I have a note here from Dr. Whidden. Let's see what it says. (Reads from a paper on which there is obviously nothing written.) 'If you and the young people of the Intermediate Department will come into the Christian Endeavour room, I think we may have a little surprise for you . . .' Well, well, well! What do you suppose it can be? (Cries of "I know, I know!" from sophisticated ones in the audience.) Maybe it is a bottle of castor-oil! (Raucous jeers from the little boys and elaborately simulated disgust on the part of the little girls.) Well, anyway, suppose we go out and see? Now if Miss Liftnagle will oblige us with a little march on the piano, we will all form a single file—"

At this point there will ensue a stampede toward the Christian Endeavour room, in which chairs will be broken, decorations demolished, and the protesting Mr. Creamer badly hurt.

This will bring to a close the first part of the entertainment.

—ROBERT BENCHLEY
Love Conquers All

It has been a troublesome time, every day with the noise of either drums, trumpets, hautboys, pipes or fiddles, some days four hundred guests, very few days under a hundred, so that, besides the vast expense, it has been very tiresome.

—LORD FERMANAGH
(Writing how glad he is that the season is over, January 12, 1712)

Why the Heaths Didn't Have This Year's Christmas Carol Program

Do you know what *afforient* is? Neither did I till I heard Priscilla,who is fifteen and who should know better, sweetly warble that she three kings afforient were, and I asked her. *Afforient,* if you are interested, is the state of being disoriented, or wandering, as one does over field and fountain, moor and mountain.

And has anybody ever wondered where the Ranger is on Christmas Eve? Well, Betsey Heath has. "*Away* is the Ranger," she will inform you, if you listen carefully. And obviously, he is away because there is no crib for his bed. After all, why should the Ranger stick around *here,* when he hasn't even got a crib much less a bed for Pete's sake!

Janet, canny little Janet, all of whose sins are premeditated and blatant, sang exactly what she intended to sing. *"No L, No L the angels did say."* It was a matter of the angels' alphabet, she explained to me a little tiredly, "A B C D E F G H I J K M N O P Q R S T U V W X Y Z. No L, *get it, Mother? No L!"* I eyed her suspiciously, because more humor in the family we do not need, but I let it pass.

Jennifer settled my next problem, which had to do with angels. Do you know how the angel of the Lord shone around? He shone around in a glowy manner, that's how. While shepherds watch'd their flock by night, she explained, the angel of the Lord came and glowy showed around. How else?

Pam, even Pam, kept announcing in her clear, sweet contralto that God and sin are reconciled, but she realized immediately, when it was pointed out to her, that God was far more likely to reconcile Himself to sinners than to sin.

Jim had to argue a little. He was the one who kept urging the shepherds to leave their "you's" and leave their "am's" and rise up, shepherds, and follow.

"What in heaven's name is this about you's and am's?" I asked him.

"Oh-h, rejection of personality, denial of self," said Jim grandly. "Practically the central thesis of Christian theology."

"I think that's Communist theory, not Christian theology," I told him. "In any case, could you come down from those philosophic heights and join us shepherds down here with our ewes (female sheep) and rams (male sheep)?"

But I was too weary to go on. "Children," I said. "Let's just do one thing absolutely *perfectly*. Let's concentrate on 'Silent Night,' because that's the one we know best anyway. Pam and Priscilla can do the alto, John can do the descant, the rest of you just sing nice and softly, and Buckley, I don't want to hear one single *note* below middle C."

They lined up, looking very clean and handsome and holy.

"Silent night, holy night," nine young voices chanted softly, and I noticed Jennifer and Betsey beginning to break up in twinkles and dimples. *"All is calm, all is bright,"* they went on, John's recorder piping low and clear. Buckley and Alison clapped their hands briefly over their mouths. *"Round John Virgin, Mother and Child,"* the chorus swelled sweetly, and I rapped hard on the piano. "Just *who*," I asked in my most restrained voice, "is Round John Virgin?"

"One of the twelve opossums," the young voices answered promptly, and they collapsed over the piano, from the piano bench into the floor, convulsed by their own delicate wit.

And that's why we didn't have this year's Christmas carol program.

—ALOÏSE BUCKLEY HEATH
National Review

It's customarily said that Christmas is done "for the kids." Considering how awful Christmas is and how little of our society likes children, this must be true.

—P. J. O'ROURKE
Modern Manners

It might do more to bring out the Christmas spirit in children to take things away from them at Christmas.

—DON HEROLD

Too much time, money, and advertising have gone into Christmas to have a small minority spoil it by going to church. . . . We're against churches remaining open on the one day of the year that is sacred to our gross national product.

—ART BUCHWALD
I Never Danced at the White House

Xmas Afterthought

The stories told of mistletoe
   are tales we herewith edit,
For each New Year's statistics show
   an overrated credit;
Tradition gives it certain fame,
   Yet wise folk buy it sparsely—
Red-blooded men react the same
   Beneath a sprig of parsley.

—WILLIAM W. PRATT

Christmas Down Our Throats

We shall soon have Christmas down our throats.

—P. G. WODEHOUSE

The Fruitcake Theory

This was the year I was going to be nice about fruit-cake. "Just try to be nice," my wife said. My younger daughter—the one who is still in high school, and talks funny—said the same thing. Actually, what she said was, "Cool it, Pops. Take a chill on the fruitcake issue." That's the same thing.

They were right. I knew they were right. It's not that I hadn't tried to be nice before. It's not my fault that some years ago I happened to pass along a theory about fruitcake I had heard from someone in Denver. The theory was that there is only one fruitcake, and that this fruitcake is simply sent on from year to year. It's just a theory.

But every year, around this time, someone calls up and says something like, "I'm doing a story on people who make fun of the holiday symbols that so many Americans hold dear—symbols that do so much for warm family life in this great country of ours and remain so very meaningful to all decent people. You're the one who maligns fruitcake, right?"

"Well, it's just a theory," I always mutter. "Something someone in Denver said once."

Who in Denver? Well, I can't remember. I'm always hearing theories from people in Denver. People in Denver are stinky with theories. I don't know why. It may be because of the altitude, although that's just a theory.

Anyway, I can't be expected to remember the name of every single person in Denver who ever laid a theory on me. I've had people in Denver tell me that if you play a certain Rolling Stones record backwards you can get detailed instructions on how to dismantle a 1973 Volkswagen Rabbit. A man I once met in a bar in Denver told me that the gases produced by the drying of all these sun-dried tomatoes were causing the Earth to wobble on its axis in a way that will put every pool table in the Western Hemisphere nearly a bubble off level by the end of this century. Don't get me started on people in Denver and their theories.

The point is that nobody ever interviews the person who gave me the theory about fruitcake, because nobody wants to start picking through this gaggle of theorymongers in Denver to find him. So I was the one called up this year by someone who said he was doing a piece about a number of Scrooge-like creatures who seemed to derive sadistic pleasure out of trashing some of our most treasured American holiday traditions.

"Well, come right over," I said. "It's always nice to be included."

He said he'd catch me the next afternoon, just after he finished interviewing a guy who never passes a Salvation Army Santa Claus without saying, "Hiya, lard-gut."

When he arrived, I remembered that I was going to try to take a chill on the fruitcake issue. I told him that the theory about there being only one fruitcake actually came from somebody in Denver—maybe the same guy who talked to me at length about his theory that dinosaurs became extinct because they couldn't adapt to the personal income tax.

Then, trying for a little historical perspective, I told him about a family in Michigan I once read about that brings out an antique fruitcake every Christmas—a fruitcake that for some reason was not eaten at Christmas dinner in 1895 and has symbolized the holidays ever since. They put it on the table, not as dessert but as something somewhere between an icon and a centerpiece. "It's a very sensible way to use a fruitcake," I said. I was trying to be nice.

"You mean you think that fruitcake would be dangerous to eat?" he asked.

"Well, you wouldn't eat an antique," I said. "My Uncle Herbert used to chew on an old sideboard now and then, but we always considered it odd behavior."

"Would a fruitcake that isn't an antique be dangerous?"

"You mean a reproduction?"

"I mean a modern fruitcake."

"There's nothing dangerous about fruitcakes as long as people send them along without eating them," I said, in the nicest sort of way. "If people ever started eating them, I suppose there might be need for federal legislation."

"How about people who buy fruitcakes for themselves?" he asked.

"Well, now that you mention it," I said, "nobody in the history of the United States has ever bought a fruitcake for himself. People have bought turnips for themselves. People have bought any number of brussels sprouts for themselves. But no one has ever bought a fruitcake for himself. That does tell you a little something about fruitcakes."

"Are you saying that everybody secretly hates fruitcakes?" he asked.

"Well, it's just a theory."

—CALVIN TRILLIN

Glorious time of great Too-Much.

—LEIGH HUNT

The making and eating of mince pies and Christmas pudding on Christmas Day is a contravention of a law passed by Cromwell's Long Parliament. It describes both dishes as "abominable and idolatrous confections to be avoided by Christians," and renders offenders subject to heavy fines, imprisonments, or both.

—*COUNTRY LIFE*

The whole Christmas buffoonery is a curse to humanity—perhaps one of the worst curses that Christianity has brought in. Growing up in a German family, I enjoyed the day—but only transiently. Before Christmas afternoon was half over I always came down with violent pains in the stomach, and usually had to be put to bed with an extra dose of castor oil. This was because at Christmas cakes and candies were on open display and might be eaten ad libitum. At all other times of the year we were on strict sanitary rations, but at Christmas it was considered only right and decent to let the children half kill themselves. I escaped death by a millimeter every Christmas day between 1884 and 1895.

—H. L. MENCKEN
(Letter to Edgar Lee Masters,
December 27, 1935)

Mrs. Hooligan's Christmas Cake

An Irish Song

As I sat in my window last evening,
　A messenger came up to me,
He had a nice neat invitation,
　Sayin' "Won't you come over to tea?"
I knew it was Hooligan sent it;
　I went for our friendship's sake,
But the very first thing that he gave me
　Was a slice of Mrs. Hooligan's cake.

Chorus: There were plums and prunes and berries,
　Raisins and currants and cinnamon, too;
There were nuts and cloves and cherries
　But the crust, it was nailed on with glue;
There were caraway seeds in abundance,
　'Twould give you a fine headache,
'Twould kill any man twice, to be eatin' a slice
　Of Mrs. Hooligan's Christmas cake!

Miss Mulligan wanted to taste it,
　But really there was no use.
She worked at it for over an hour,
　But couldn't get a slice of it loose;
Then Joe went out for a hatchet
　And Jerry came in with a saw,

But that cake was enough, be th' horrors!
   To paralyze anyone's jaw!

Chorus: There were plums and prunes and berries,
etc.

—ANONYMOUS

Not So Calm, Not So Bright

Officially it's Christmastide
As shoppers, duly fortified
With Libriums or Tylenols,
Descend upon congested malls
And hark as herald angels sing,
And burly Ives and bygone Bing,
In tones so loud I understand
They echo to the Holy Land,
Reverberating on that height
That once enjoyed a *Silent* Night.

—BOB McKENTY

Confound You, December Twenty-Sixth, I Apologize

December twenty-fifth is an exciting day because it
   is what people refer to when Merry Christmas
   they wish you;
But December twenty-sixth is just the day you
   spend tripping over ribbons and wading through
   green and scarlet tissue.
It is a day of such anticlimax as to frustrate the most
   ambitious,
It is lined with gray satin like a medium-priced
   casket, its atmosphere is faintly morticious.
It is a day oppressive as asthma,
A day on which you want to call up the blood bank
   and ask them to return your plasma.
Its hours are as dilatory
As a ten-cent depilatory.
Indeed it is a day subject to such obsecration and
   obloquy
That I am beginning to feel sorry for it, my knees
   are getting wobloquy as I strangle a sobloquy.
I am regretful that in discussing the reputation of
   December twenty-sixth I may have said anything
   to jeopardize it,
So by way of making amends I suggest that from

now on we not necessarily lionize it, but couldn't
we maybe just leopardize it?

—OGDEN NASH

The Night After Christmas

'Twas the night *after* Christmas, and all through the
    home
Raged a terrible headache whenever you'd roam.

The house looked a wreck. There were signs
    everywhere
To prove to the world that St. Nick had been
    there.

The children were still having fun with their toys,
And breaking all records for long-sustained noise,

When out in the hall there arose such a clatter,
I opened the door to see what was the matter.

And what to my wondering eyes should appear,
But a man in distress and devoid of good cheer.

He lay on the floor of the corridor narrow,
And out of the small of his back stuck an arrow!

It had come from the bow of his own little lad.
I knew in a moment it must be poor dad!

I rushed for the phone, and had just turned around
When mother crashed into the room with a bound,

Pursued by a child with a rifle. Oh, well,
It seems that to please him she played William
    Tell.

The apple was okay, but mother was not.
There wasn't a shadow of doubt she'd been shot.

The kid was still shooting his air gun—how merry!
He yelled, "Play some more, ma! It's funny, ma,
    very!"

Behind him came Willie, the boy from next door.
He carried a sword and he yelled, "Let's play war!"

He rode on a broom, took a wild swing at me
And carved quite a strip from the cap of my knee.

Then out of his room tottered old Uncle Lew,
His arm in a sling and one leg, I think, too.

He'd helped little Oscar try out his new sled,
And had quite a gash on the top of his head.

He'd also been playing with Ethelbert's skis,
And murmured quite weakly, "The ambulance,
    please!"

Next grandpa came wallowing out of the bath
(I never had seen any man in such wrath).

He looked all awash. He was all dripping wet.
His clothes were all soused. He was angry, you bet!

It served him quite right. Any man is a dub
When he tries to sail children's toy boats in the
 tub!

I stood there aghast when, no fooling, Aunt Nell
Swooped through on a kiddy-car, going pell-mell.

She upset the tree. There were sparks from a wire.
I knew in an instant the house was on fire!

Then things went all black, and when next I came
 to,
I was out on the lawn with a pullmotor crew.

The house was still burning, the kids, little dears!
Were dancing and shouting, and giving three
 cheers.

The fire chief stood by and completed his work.
He snickered a bit, then he turned with a jerk.

Laying a finger aside of his nose,
And, giving a nod, he said, "Roll up the hose!"

He jumped in his car, sounded siren and whistle,
And away he then flew like the down from a
 thistle.

And I heard him exclaim to his smoke-eating boys,
"Well, adults *will* play with kids' Christmas toys!"

—H. I. PHILLIPS
The New York Sun, December 26, 1935

Farewell, Noel

'Twas the day after Christmas and all through the
　　mall
Not a carol was heard that had blared
　　throughout fall.
The Salvation Army was furloughed, I guess,
And reindeer had flown to another address.
The tannenbaum's felled and the mistletoe
　　missing,
With malcontent shoppers in no mood for
　　kissing.
The *crèche* is in storage; the Virgin released, her
Floor space relinquished to fashions for Easter,
For as 'twas with Christmas, without rhyme or
　　reason,
The stores rush another liturgical season.
While, sheeplike, the People of God (every one!)
Queue up at "Exchanges," *Redemption*'s begun.

—BOB McKENTY

106 · CHRISTMAS DOWN OUR THROATS

Visions of Poly-Plums Dance in My Head

With plastic Christmas gone its way
We'll turn again to everyday.
The poly-holly we'll unsnap
From frames and fixtures, then we'll wrap
The plastic swags and berry wreath,
And in a dust-proof plastic sheath
We'll shield the never-dying tree
Until next year's Nativity.
We'll roll the big red plastic bow
That decked the door; the mistletoe
We'll bend and stash for future use,
And should the berries jostle loose
We'll plastic-glue them on next year
When we haul out our deathless cheer.

—JOY NIMNON KRAUS

In the

Manner

of . . .

Christmas Afternoon

Done in the Manner, if Not the Spirit, of Dickens

What an afternoon! Mr. Gummidge said that, in his estimation, there never had *been* such an afternoon since the world began, a sentiment which was heartily endorsed by Mrs. Gummidge and all the little Gummidges, not to mention the relatives who had come over from Jersey for the day.

In the first place, there was the *ennui*. And such *ennui* as it was! A heavy, overpowering *ennui*, such as results from a participation in eight courses of steaming, gravied food, topping off with salted nuts which the little old spinster Gummidge from Oak Hill said she never knew when to stop eating—and true enough she didn't—a dragging, devitalizing *ennui*, which left its victims strewn about the living room in various attitudes of prostration suggestive of those of the petrified occupants in a newly unearthed Pompeiian dwelling; an *ennui* which carried with it a retinue of yawns, snarls and thinly veiled insults, and which ended in ruptures in the clan spirit serious enough to last throughout the glad new year.

Then there were the toys! Three and a quarter dozen toys to be divided among seven children. Surely enough, you or I might say, to satisfy the little tots. But that would be because we didn't know the tots. In came Baby Lester Gummidge, Lillian's boy, dragging an electric grain-elevator which happened to be the only toy in the entire collection that appealed to little Norman, five-year-old son of Luther, who lived in Rahway. In came curly-headed Effie in frantic and throaty disputation with Arthur, Jr., over the possession of an articulated zebra. In came Everett, bearing a mechanical negro which would no longer dance, owing to a previous forcible feeding by the baby of a marshmallow into its only available aperture. In came Fonlansbee, teeth buried in the hand of little Ormond, who bore a popular but battered remnant of what had once been the proud false bosom of a hussar's uniform. In they all came, one after another, some crying, some snapping, some pulling, some pushing—all appealing to their respective parents for aid in their intramural warfare.

And the cigar smoke! Mrs. Gummidge said that she didn't mind the smoke from a good cigarette, but would they mind if she opened the windows for just a minute in order to clear the room of the heavy aroma of used cigars? Mr. Gummidge stoutly maintained that they were good cigars. His brother, George Gummidge, said that he, likewise, would say that they were.

At which colloquial sally both Gummidge brothers laughed testily, thereby breaking the laughter record for the afternoon.

Aunt Libbie, who lived with George, remarked from the dark corner of the room that it seemed just like Sunday to her. An amendment was offered to this statement by the cousin, who was in the insurance business, stating that it was worse than Sunday. Murmurings indicative of as hearty agreement with this sentiment as their lethargy would allow came from the other members of the family circle, causing Mr. Gummidge to suggest a walk in the air to settle their dinner.

And then arose such a chorus of protestations as has seldom been heard. It was too cloudy to walk. It was too raw. It looked like snow. It looked like rain. Luther Gummidge said that he must be starting along home soon, anyway, bringing forth the acid query from Mrs. Gummidge as to whether or not he was bored. Lillian said that she felt a cold coming on, and added that something they had had for dinner must have been undercooked. And so it went, back and forth, forth and back, up and down, and in and out, until Mr. Gummidge's suggestion of a walk in the air was reduced to a tattered impossibility and the entire company glowed with ill-feeling.

In the meantime, we must not forget the children. No one else could. Aunt Libbie said that she didn't think there was anything like children to make a Christmas; to which Uncle Ray, the one with the Masonic fob, said, "No, thank God!" Although Christmas is supposed to be the season of good cheer, you (or I, for that matter) couldn't have told, from listening to the little ones, but what it was the children's Armageddon season, when Nature had decreed that only the fittest should survive, in order that the race might be carried on by the strongest, the most predatory and those possessing the best protective coloring. Although there were constant admonitions to Fonlansbee to "Let Ormond have that whistle now; it's his," and to Arthur, Jr., not to be selfish, but to "give the kiddie-car to Effie; she's smaller than you are," the net result was always that Fonlansbee kept the whistle and Arthur, Jr., rode in permanent, albeit disputed, possession of the kiddie-car. Oh, that we mortals should set ourselves up against the inscrutable workings of Nature!

Hallo! A great deal of commotion! That was Uncle George stumbling over the electric train which had early in the afternoon ceased to function and which had been left directly across the threshold. A great deal of crying! That was Arthur, Jr., bewailing the destruction of his already useless train, about which he had forgotten until the present moment. A great deal of recrimination! That was Arthur, Sr., and George fixing it up. And finally a great crashing! That was Baby

Lester pulling over the tree on top of himself, necessitating the bringing to bear of all of Uncle Ray's knowledge of forestry to extricate him from the wreckage.

And finally Mrs. Gummidge passed the Christmas candy around. Mr. Gummidge afterward admitted that this was a tactical error on the part of his spouse. I no more believe that Mrs. Gummidge thought they wanted that Christmas candy than I believe that she thought they wanted the cold turkey which she later suggested. My opinion is that she wanted to drive them home. At any rate, that is what she succeeded in doing. Such cries as there were of "Ugh! Don't let me see another thing to eat!" and "Take it away!" Then came hurried scramblings in the coat-closet for overshoes. There were the rasping sounds made by cross parents when putting wraps on children. There were insincere exhortations to "come and see us soon" and to "get together for lunch some time." And, finally, there were slammings of doors and the silence of utter exhaustion, while Mrs. Gummidge went about picking up stray sheets of wrapping paper.

And, as Tiny Tim might say in speaking of Christmas afternoon as an institution, "God help us, every one."

—ROBERT BENCHLEY
The Benchley Roundup

We Three Clods from Omaha Are

*Sung to the Tune of "We Three Kings
from Orient Are"*

We three clods from Omaha are
Spending Christ-mas Eve in a car;
    Driving, drinking,
    Glasses clinking—
Who needs a lousy bar?
Oh-h-h-h—

Drink to Charlie, drink to Paul,
Drink to friends we can't recall;
    Swerving, speeding,
    Signs unheeding—
Drink to anything at all.

We three clods are feeling no pain,
Drunk as skunks with booze on the brain;
    Senses losing,
    Till we're cruising
Into a wrong-way lane.
Oh-h-h-h—

Drink to Melvin, drink to Fred,
Drink to those two trucks ahead;
    Headlights flashing,

Screeching, crashing—
Drink till they pronounce us dead.

—FRANK JACOBS
Mad

A Visit from Saint Nicholas
(In the Ernest Hemingway Manner)

It was the night before Christmas. The house was very quiet. No creatures were stirring in the house. There weren't even any mice stirring. The stockings had been hung carefully by the chimney. The children hoped that Saint Nicholas would come and fill them.

The children were in their beds. Their beds were in the room next to ours. Mamma and I were in our beds. Mamma wore a kerchief. I had my cap on. I could hear the children moving. We didn't move. We wanted the children to think we were asleep.

"Father," the children said.

There was no answer. He's there, all right, they thought.

"Father," they said, and banged on their beds.

"What do you want?" I asked.

"We have visions of sugarplums," the children said.

"Go to sleep," said mamma.

"We can't sleep," said the children. They stopped talking, but I could hear them moving. They made sounds.

"Can you sleep?" asked the children.

"No," I said.

"You ought to sleep."

"I know. I ought to sleep."

"Can we have some sugarplums?"

"You can't have any sugarplums," said mamma.

"We just asked you."

There was a long silence. I could hear the children moving again.

"Is Saint Nicholas asleep?" asked the children.

"No," mamma said. "Be quiet."

"What the hell would he be asleep tonight for?" I asked.

"He might be," the children said.

"He isn't," I said.

"Let's try to sleep," said mamma.

The house became quiet once more. I could hear the rustling noises the children made when they moved in their beds.

Out on the lawn a clatter arose. I got out of bed and went to the window. I opened the shutters; then I threw up the sash. The moon shone on the snow. The moon gave the luster of mid-day to objects in the snow. There was a miniature sleigh in the snow, and eight tiny reindeer. A little man was driving them. He was lively and quick. He whistled and shouted at the reindeer and called them by their names. Their names were Dasher, Dancer, Prancer, Vixen, Comet, Cupid, Donder, and Blitzen.

He told them to dash away to the top of the porch, and then he told them to dash away to the top of the wall. They did. The sleigh was full of toys.

"Who is it?" mamma asked.

"Some guy," I said. "A little guy."

I pulled my head in out of the window and listened. I heard the reindeer on the roof. I could hear their hoofs pawing and prancing on the roof. "Shut the window," said mamma. I stood still and listened.

"Reindeer," I said. I shut the window and walked about. It was cold. Mamma sat up in the bed and looked at me.

"How would they get on the roof?" mamma asked.

"They fly."

"Get into bed. You'll catch cold."

Mamma lay down in bed. I didn't get into bed. I kept walking around.

"What do you mean, they fly?" asked mamma.

"Just fly is all."

Mamma turned away toward the wall. She didn't say anything.

I went out into the room where the chimney was. The little man came down the chimney and stepped into the room. He was dressed all in fur. His clothes were covered with ashes and soot from the chimney. On his back was a pack like a peddler's pack. There were toys in it. His cheeks and nose were red and he had dimples. His eyes twinkled. His mouth was little, like a bow, and his beard was very white. Between his teeth was a stumpy pipe. The smoke from the pipe encircled his head in a wreath. He laughed and his belly shook. It shook like a bowl of red jelly. I laughed. He winked his eye, then he gave a twist to his head. He didn't say anything.

He turned to the chimney and filled the stockings and turned away from the chimney. Laying his fingers aside his nose, he gave a nod. Then he went up the chimney and looked up. I saw him get into his sleigh. He whistled at his team and the team flew away. The team flew as lightly as thistledown. The driver called out, "Merry Christmas and good night." I went back to bed.

"What was it?" asked mamma. "Saint Nicholas?" She smiled.

"Yeah," I said.

She sighed and turned in the bed.

"I saw him," I said.

"Sure."

"I did see him."

"Sure you saw him." She turned farther toward the wall.

"Father," said the children.

"There you go," mamma said. "You and your flying reindeer."

"Go to sleep," I said.

"Can we see Saint Nicholas when he comes?" the children asked.

"You got to be asleep," I said. "You got to be asleep when he comes. You can't see him unless you're unconscious."

"Father knows," mamma said.

I pulled the covers over my mouth. It was warm under the covers. As I went to sleep I wondered if mamma was right.

—JAMES THURBER
Collecting Himself

Dear Father Christmas

*(A parody of Dylan Thomas,
A Child's Christmas in Wales)*

Dear Sir, I was born and brought up in one of those steep-sided, smoky little industrial zinc baths. Life was hard then, it smelled of carbolic and clanged when you kicked it. But we were happy, living out our double-breasted days in the hobbledy house full of Olympic mice and gravy-boat-grabbing aunts, and we waited for Christmas, when I would help my mother knead and pummel and funnel and mince my father—oh, and her geological Welsh cakes, her marzipan, green as weeds, and marvelous, confusing, runny sausages. Mam, with her porcelain features, watering eyes and floury arms, sounded like a vase upside down, and looked worse, but to poor, drunken Uncle Ernie she was priest and comforter, bag and baggage, lock, stock and bottle opener. Every time he came into the room, Bass-breathed, beacon-nosed, his eyes like two ball-bearings discovered in a pizza, she would stand up, and try to get him to do the same, but Ernie always declined, sometimes quite suddenly, and I would creep away and sit alone, outside in the giant, neighbor-needling hutch Dad had build, needlessly alas, to house the Roget's Thesaurus he had heard of me winning for a prize at school in Cwmclogdans Road.

Listen. Listen. Listen, you prodigal old toy-to-taller, you whimsical bearded typhoon, I can go on all night like this. The thing is, do you ever call at the University of Texas? If so, will you kindly drop this off, see if they're interested, tell them there's plenty more, and bringing me, say 95 percent of any fee? Thanks. Also can you lend me three guineas till next

Christmas? The doctor has told me the shadow on my
lung is caused by an empty wallet. Oh the pain oh
                              Yours very truly,

                              —RUSSELL DAVIES

Dear Father Christmas

(A Parody of W. H. Auden)

I

Dear Father Christmas. What are you bringing
Over the rooftops of Oxford winging?

Crackers for the mad, boaters for the Seine,
A drop of the hard stuff, a choo-choo train.

Zipping past Balliol, a shower of sparks
The porter's collie-dog, Prurient, barks

Past coffee-bars and ancient tuckshops
Peeping through windows of red-lit brothels

"Look at Merton," Santa hollers,
"Silent miles of toil-bent scholars."

Statues awaken as on he races,
Peep from niches at his Day-Glo braces.

A startled owl stops dead in its tracks
And gets knocked cold by the flying sacks.

In the Ashmolean, never a word
But on the roof slops a reindeer turd.

II

Dawn threatens. Is Santa done?
Down towards Reading he inclines
Towards the Third Division of the Football League
Towards the feel of Lux-lene curtains, the new
    settees
Set on the foam-back like reclining hippos.
All Berkshire waits for him:
In Suburb, setee of the plain,
Men long for socks.

III

Stockings of green, stockings obscene,
Stockings that smell and swell as well,
Abysmal stripe and ghastly tartan
Hairy calf-length, anklet spartan,
"Product of Italy," "Made in Dumbarton,"
Wrapped in a tissue, sealed in a carton,
" 'Never without 'em,' says E. Lustgarten."
Hose enjoyable, hose unemployable,

Tights giving too much room for the kneecaps
Tights kitted out with rude-looking pee-flaps
Tights for the winter, ballet and sex,
Tights where the spot is marked with an X,
Thick tights for journeyers, thicker for hernias,
Knitted in nylon of every shade
The puce, the indigo, orange and jade,
The knotty, the spotty, the been-to-the-menders,
The very hard-wearing from Marks and Suspenders,
See-through, stay-fresh, tweed or twee,
The limp and the lumpy and the just-not-me.

IV

Millions are still abed
Dreaming of mollifying taxmen
Or a friendly feel behind the shelves in stock-room
      or store-room:
Abed in working Reading, working in well-read
      Oxford,
Reading in Welwyn Garden City,
They continue their snooze,
But shall wake soon and nudge their neighbor
And none will play at postman's knock
Without a heartening of the quick.
For who can bear to feel himself
At Christmas?
   Yours documentarily,
   W. H. AUDEN (master)

P.S. I hope you agree with me that this is worth an extra bottle of Elizabeth Arden Crow's-Foot Creme this Xmas, you old stinge.

—RUSSELL DAVIES

Christmas

In Japan Christmas is known as Easter. In China it is known as Election Day, or Yong Kip Pur.

This is the time of year when we want to recapture memories of Christmases past by rereading that ever fresh Dickens classic, the—the—oh, you know the one. As long as English is our mother tongue that tale will not be forgotten, with its recital of how Christmas came to the Wigg household.

Who can forget the description of Mrs. Wigg busily preparing for the glorious morrow, assisted with unwonted and tremendous gusto by a bevy of little Wiggs, or Wiggettes. Never have children been so suddenly and unaccountably industrious, it seems.

"Oh, mother," shouts little Fenella Wigg, "how happy I am when I think that father has promised not to come home tight tonight!"

And the cynicism of her sister Madge.

"Don't take any odds on pa not coming home tight," she advises.

In comes Perkin Wigg, "man of the family" at fourteen, who has stopped in McCloskey's place to get a couple of "shots." He reports the presence there of Wigg *père,* blotto.

And the grand climax, when, as the family is steeped in gloom over the dismal prospect, Wigg *père* enters all in a glow and shouts cheerily that no Christmas tree will be needed because he is all lit up. At which sally every one laughs and they have a jolly Christmas, after all.

Dear old tale!

At Christmas time those who have should remember those who have not. One way in which we who are more fortunate can help is by saving our used Christmas trees for distribution among needy families. In cases where the husband and father is not working for some such reason as aversion these meaty old evergreens serve a useful end. They make excellent whittling material wherewith he may while away the long hours of the day until mother and the children get home from work to cook his supper.

Ah, the preparations for Christmas in a big city like New York. The bustle, the confusion of it all. Who said bustles had gone out of style?

How the spirit of it gets into one's blood! How even the most cynical is engulfed in the flood of warmth and good feeling that comes with the Yuletide! Old grievances are forgotten. People take on a kindly aspect. Faces that would be quite a trial during other seasons, such as Lent, are quite possible now, suffused as they are by a kindly glow that softens the features which stray over their visages indiscriminately and not always in the best of taste.

What a good-natured, jostling crowd at the railroad stations, where New Yorkers are trying to get Pullman seats on trains leaving for their old homes. The rubicund ticket agent glows as you ask him if he has two chairs for Albany on the 12:25.

"Naw," he answers.

You love him for the cheery note in his voice.

There is much good-natured banter between people who are in line and others who want to wedge themselves into a place up near the head of the queue.

"Come on, come on, get back to the end of the line," cry those who have been waiting to the mischievous intruders.

"Aw, so's your old man," is the ready retort of the culprits, given with true Yulish heartiness.

Crowds everywhere and much gay picking of pockets. The poor pickpockets! They have to work like nailers during the holiday season. No wonder so many of them crack under the strain and start taking drugs in one form or another.

*　　*　　*

Something should be done, too, about the various poor families at Christmas time.

I know a poor woman, mother of sixteen children, who worries terribly over the situation at Christmas.

"Look at them," she told me last Christmas Eve, indicating with a despairing gesture a pile of forty Christmas dinners in the corner. "What am I going to do with them? Where am I going to put them all?"

As she spoke charity workers came in with four more Christmas baskets and the poor lady swooned.

The day after Christmas is called Tidying-Up Day. It is the day when we must inevitably face the many problems that crop up after Christmas. Let us not shirk them but face them manfully, for that is half the battle, and half a battle is better than none.

How shall we get the drum away from Junior—the drum that Uncle Will gave him? Good old Will, always the kindly, thoughtful Will; always thinking of somebody else, always giving drums to Junior at Christmas. Let us all express our love for Uncle Will by stamping on him good and hard the first time we catch him lying on the floor.

We can't take the drum forcibly from Junior. We tried to do that Christmas before last, didn't we? And look at poor grandpa, still on crutches! We tried hiding the drum on Junior. We tried hiding Junior. The day after last Christmas father drove twenty miles out into the country with Junior, and after tying a good heavy millstone around his little legs dropped him into Fisher's Pond, but he was back the next day.

How then to get the drum away from Junior, for we must separate him from it, else grandmother will be having delusions of grandeur, papa will become a manic-depressive, Cousin Elsie will be a psychoneurotic, grandpa will get that feeling of impending disaster and I, who constitute the meal ticket for the whole gang, will not be able to escape a recurrence of the old dementia praecox.

Let us do the thing sensibly. Let us quietly and without ostentation pack Junior off tomorrow for a month's visit with Uncle Will.

Junior shall visit Uncle Will, taking with him his precious drum. But we must do the thing right. Suppose Junior should break his drum while visiting Uncle Will. Suppose one of Uncle Will's great big, hobnailed brogans should accidentally come down on Junior's drum. Junior without a drum? Horrible thought!

Our course is clear. We shall leave orders with the drum company to leave a fresh drum every morning at Uncle Will's while Junior is there.

Today also sees the plum pudding restored to its hiding place in the attic, there to await the advent of another Yule. No accessory of the Christmastide gets or deserves more of our affection than the old family plum pudding. Some of these puddings have done service in families for over a hundred years.

In "ye olden dayes" the plum pudding was often hauled forth at divers times during the year to do yeoman service in case some belligerent feudal lord attacked his neighbor's castle. Dropped upon the assailant's head from the ramparts of the beleaguered stronghold, the plum pudding, like the Northwest Mounted Police, always "got its man." Generally it could be recovered before it had rolled too far. Sometimes the head of the attacking earl or lord proved too much for the poor pudding, which thereupon broke. This was considered an ill omen, by the earl.

The Standard Oil Company does not throw away its useless Christmas presents as it formerly did. A clever chemist in the company's employ discovered that useful by-products can be made from Christmas presents which formerly were considered fit only for the ash-heap, or to give to poor relations next Christmas. Did you know that eighty percent of the coke consumed in the United States is made from Christmas cigars?

Save the wishbone of the turkey, too, and ask your friends to give you theirs. When you have gathered a thousand of these little trinkets you will find that they make an attractive little border for the kitchen garden in place of the old-fashioned clam shell.

—FRANK SULLIVAN
Innocent Bystanding

Dashing Through the Dough

—RALPH M. WEYSER

A bribe with bells.

—JOHN STEINBECK

The Christmas cooing is followed by the January billing.

—ANONYMOUS

The Christmas season has come to mean the period when the public plays Santa Claus to the merchants.

—JOHN ANDREW HOLMES
Wisdom in Small Doses

Each Christmas season the economists say that the improvement in business is due to holiday buying. You can't beat these economic experts for sharp analysis.

—ANONYMOUS

I believed in Christmas until I was eight years old. I had saved up some money carrying ice in Philadelphia, and was going to buy my mother a copper-bottomed clothes boiler for Christmas. I kept the money hidden in a brown crock in the coal bin. My father found the crock. He did exactly what I would have done in his place. He stole the money. And ever since then I've remembered nobody on Christmas, and I want nobody to remember me either.

—W. C. FIELDS

Christmas is a time when kids tell Santa what they want and adults pay for it. Deficits are when adults tell the government what they want—and their kids pay for it.

—RICHARD LAMM
*(When governor of Colorado,
to National League of Cities)*

Christmas should be celebrated on the birthday of Jesse James.

—DON HEROLD

Treed!

Setting out to buy a Christmas tree is one of those warm communal ceremonies that enfold one in a mist of good feelings for one's neighborhood, one's solid place in life. Look at me, the provider, bringing home the Christmas tree to the family. One embraces the tree as another of those cherished Christmas traditions like wrapping the presents, and shredding your fingers trying to put small Japanese appliances together. As annual ceremony, Getting the Christmas Tree ranks right up there with Filling Out Your Tax Return at the Last Possible Moment, and the Annual Visit to the Dentist.

Every year I swear it's the last time I'll get a Christmas tree and every year I get conned into buying one. Last fall, in what I thought was an inspired piece of sabotage, I "mistakenly" sold the Christmas tree stand at a yard sale.

This Christmas, notwithstanding the lack of a tree stand, She Who Is Never to Be Brooked and the Young Tyrant grimly insisted that I get out there to the marketplace and buy a tree. No tree, no dinner.

I've always been opposed to Christmas trees, I suspect because the ceremonial Christmas trees in the reception halls or refectories of the various orphanages in which I spent my gilded youth, had piles of gaily wrapped, false presents underneath their branches, arranged in artfully tumbled piles to suggest a Great Potlatch waiting for us early on Christmas morning. Alas, none of those empty boxes were ever opened or handed out. No doubt they were carefully put away for the following year. My earliest memory of the Christmas tree is therefore charged with a feeling of betrayal, of deception, of false promise. On the other hand it was great training for the real world lying in wait for us just outside those orphanage doors.

Then too I've always felt that the cutting down of an evergreen and the disfiguring of it with bits of colored glass and shreds of plastic is a barbarous custom. I'm told the practice originated with some benighted Jute or Gothic tribe back in the Middle Ages. And I wouldn't want to know what those berserkers originally decorated their trees with—probably various small body parts of their enemies. Anyway, why follow the customs of a people whose idea of a good time was to paint themselves blue and howl the night away under lightning-blasted oak trees? With people who actually prayed to a parasite, the mistletoe? And expected answers?

Nevertheless, at the last possible moment on Christmas Eve, I was ordered to stop sniveling and be a mensch and manfully take my part in the annual Fleecing of the Innocents ceremony. Harried out of the house, I stumbled forth into the bitter cold to face humiliation yet again.

"What do I have for twenty bucks?" the tree stand assistant repeated, with a who-needs-this-cheapskate? sneer. I'm convinced the sinister churls who work Christmas tree lots are actually engaged in some sort of initiation rite imposed on potential Mafia recruits.

"They *start* at thirty-five. Well, there's that beheaded dwarf over there for twenty-five. That is, if you want to spend a couple of hours wiring the branches into some sort of shape. You could always stick something big up there to make a top, like an upside down wastebasket, ha, ha. No, I couldn't give you a reduction. Better take what you get or you'll end up with nothing."

I take what I get, drag it home and modestly endure the traditional paeans of congratulation.

"No, it's really nice except why is there such a big gap on one side?" "They didn't have trees with tops on them?" "How come the needles are so dull?" "Have you been drinking again?"

Christmas trees. Bah, humbug! Move over, Scrooge, and pour me a mug of that bitter grog.

—ARTHUR ROTH

'Twas the month after Christmas
And Santa had flit;
Came there tidings for father
Which read: "Please remit!"

—ANONYMOUS

Christmas Lights on Yonge Street

You've seen all the colored lights
they hang up over Yonge Street
now at every Christmas time?

Paid for by local businessmen,
they say you can tell each night
how good the day's take has been.

If they seem to shine very green
the dollars were rolling in.
If the color's a darker red,
then it was slow, very slow.

So shine with your greedy shine,
Christmas lights of Yonge Street,
under a cash-or-credit sky!

—RAYMOND SOUSTER

Christmas Madrigal

Hail, Noel, the season jolly!
   Tra-la-la-la-la! Tra-la-la-la!
Ho for the tree, the wreath, the holly!
   Tra-la-la-la-la! Tra-la-la-la!
Ho for the Yule log burning merry!
Ho for the warming Tom and Jerry!
Ho for the toys in tinseled wrappings!
Ho for the children's happy yappings!
Ho for a gift to please my Honey!
Ho for the . . . HEY! . . . I'm short of money!
. . . WHOA . . . . . . !!!

—JOSEPH S. NEWMAN
Verse Yet! World Pub. Co.

Ode to My Bank Account on Christmas Day

I saw thirty bills come mailing in, mailing in,
   On Christmas Day, on Christmas Day.

I saw thirty bills come mailing in, mailing in.
    And each one said: Time to pay! Time to pay.
On Christmas Day in the morning.

—LOUIS PHILLIPS

An Old-Fashioned Christmas

I like an old-fashioned Christmas
With turkey and dressing
Eaten at Grandma's house
With Gramps asking the blessing,
Then carols sung in the parlor
How the memory thrills!
But the thing I like best
About an old-fashioned Christmas
Is remembering the bills.

Toboggan $2.98
Pr gloves 98
Sweater $1.98
3 pr sox 98
Tax 0

—MILDRED LUTON

Index of Contributors